Stella Stillson Slaughter, B. S., M. A.

Formerly Director of Division of Education of Exceptional Children, Milwaukee State Teachers College, University of Wisconsin at Milwaukee, and Supervisor of Special Classes, State of Wisconsin Department of Public Instruction.

The Educable

Mentally Retarded Child

and

His Teacher

 F. A. DAVIS COMPANY, PHILADELPHIA

© 1964 by F. A. Davis Company

Second Printing, October 1966
Third Printing, July 1972

Library of Congress Catalog Card Number 64-20819

ISBN 0-8036-7890-8

This book is dedicated to all teachers of mentally retarded children who are striving to help these children attain their optimum of happiness, independence, and responsibility.

Preface

This book has been written as a textbook for teachers and prospective teachers of the mentally retarded, and those interested in the educational procedures to be employed in their training. It is not a source of general information about the education of the mentally retarded; rather, it is a child-centered book that places emphasis upon the mentally retarded child as an individual. It attempts to define for the teacher his own relationship, and to indicate his responsibilities, to the pupil. It places the teacher in the position of a guardian of rights and morals, not just a conveyor of subject matter or an instructor of skills.

The book is intended to help the teacher look upon the individual retarded child as an integral human whole. As the child's limitations are recognized by the teacher, his potentialities should be equally acknowledged. While training the child to cope as bravely and as efficiently as he can with the demands that society will impose upon him, the teacher should protect him from situations which would exact more than he has to give. The only way to teach a child to meet his problems of the future is by giving him practice in meeting problems of the present, and the proficiency of the teacher will be tested by his or her ability to see the child as an adult of the future and to set problems that bear relationship to it. While the satisfaction of less permanent needs may serve as stepping stones to more permanent ones, the teacher should be able to discern the difference between transitory and lasting needs. Throughout the book stress has been placed upon the necessity for seeing the child as a part of his environment. The child is the product of his native structure and native abilities and of the influences that his environment exerts upon them. His curriculum should emanate from his environment. He should be taught how to advantageously control it, conforming when conformation is called for, and changing or resisting when change or resistance is to be preferred. He should be fortified as well as he can against the likelihood of defeat by his environment, and should be prepared to live as successfully as he can within it.

Rather than appending a lengthy bibliography the author has chosen to be selective in her suggestions for reading. A few references of general informational nature, that well supplement each other in their content and carry extensive bibliographies, have been appended. It is not intended to suggest that a teacher unnecessarily curtail her professional reading, but it is hoped that from the wealth of books and articles that have been written about mental retardation and its implications, he or she will wisely choose those that seem most likely to influence thinking, best answer problems, and purposively activate teaching.

STELLA S. SLAUGHTER

Table of Contents

1/

The Educable
Mental Retardate

Significance of the term "educable" as applied to the mental retardate. The term "educable" is applied to those mentally retarded children possessed of native potentialities that will, other things being equal, permit them to become integrated into society with a relative degree of maturity of action. The degree will be conditioned to a considerable extent by the educational opportunities afforded, as well as the environment of which these children are, or will become, a part and to which they must respond.

The IQ's of educable retardates. Psychologists agree that the diagnosis of mental retardation should not be based solely on the IQ (intelligence quotient). However, the IQ's obtained on well standardized intelligence tests bear a positive relationship to academic success and school progress. In most public school classes for the educable mentally retarded, only those children within certain IQ limitations are permitted entrance. The usual range of IQ's is from 50 to 70 or 75, and in some instances 80.

The reliability of the IQ as a prediction of success in school subjects. While as implied above there is a positive relationship between the IQ and mastery of the common school subjects, it cannot be assumed that children of like IQ's will show equal facility of learning about any one subject, nor will ultimate degrees of accomplishment be the same. One child with an IQ of 60 may be a much better reader than another child of like IQ. It may be assumed that no mentally retarded child will be able to cope with the complexities of trigonometry, but it cannot be predicted just how difficult may be the problems in adding and subtracting, multiplying and dividing he may be able to solve. However, when at any given mental level there is a wide discrepancy between his own and average accomplishments in any school subject of importance, an earnest effort should be made to locate and correct any controllable and remediable factors which might account for his discrepancies in learning.

Limitations of the IQ as a measurement of abilities. There are many significant abilities of which the IQ is no prognosticator. There are many aptitudes which are not highly correlated with general intelligence. Motor skills and mechanical abilities are not measured by the general intelligence test. The IQ certainly cannot be relied upon to inform a teacher about a child's personality traits. The IQ cannot be depended upon to predict with any degree of accuracy the social maturity an educable mental retardate may eventually attain, because he may often be trained to perform socially much more maturely than he reads or writes or ciphers.

Common characteristics of mental retardates. Mental retardates differ as widely in their manner of behaving as do children in general. While there is no set of personality traits that may be regarded as belonging to retardates alone, there are certain inferiorities that are shared by retardates in general. The retardate learns slowly. His ability to comprehend is limited. His reasoning is relatively weak. His ability to generalize is below par. He is relatively limited in his ability to meet the exigencies of complex or strange situations. Not all retardates, even those of like IQ's, will be equally deficient in these respects, but mentally retarded individuals in general fall below norm in them. It must be added that the inferiorities may be the accompaniments of conditions other than mental retardation.

Physical conditions accompanying mental retardation. There are certain physical ailments which are often, but not necessarily, accompanied by mental retardation. For example, an individual with cerebral palsy may or may not be mentally retarded, depending upon what brain areas beyond those that control motor coordination are affected; or the crippled condition of a mental retardate may bear no causative relationship to his retardation. Whatever the cause, the child with a disabling physical condition may need therapy to alleviate or better the condition, or to minimize the disabling effects upon his development and activities. If a mentally retarded child is also physically handicapped, his training and education should take cognizance of the effect of his physical disability upon his learning opportunities. Such teaching adjustments as are necessary to enable him to make the most of his potentialities should be made.

Educable retardates who react abnormally. In a class of mentally retarded, there may be one or more children who seem unable to benefit from usually effective methods of teaching. What may stimulate the majority of the group in a manner favorable to their growth and development may prove to be overstimulating and educationally ineffective for certain children. A child may even react in some seemingly senseless manner. A child may try to react to various stimuli at the same time with resulting confusion. A child may seem unable to shift from one pattern to another—he may follow the same pattern over and over for no apparent good reason. Many of these unstable children are in the category of brain-injured children. The brain-damage may result from one or more numerous causes. Knowledges about the origin and nature of a child's difficulties may have direct bearing upon teaching methods to be employed. Unless already authoritatively informed about a child whose behavior is abnormal the teacher should employ every ethical means to obtain a clinical diagnosis and directions for his care and training. The teacher's judgment must be relied upon to distinguish between the temper tantrums and misbehaviors which may be psychologically accounted for as the result of faulty and unwise conditioning, and the abnormal behavior induced by internal causes.

The culturally deprived child. Sometimes a child's educational retardation may be due to the fact that he has been denied the cultural experiences which bear relationship to school progress. It is quite commonly agreed that the individual who has spent his early life in an impoverished environment may be expected to have a lower IQ than if he had lived in a culturally rich environment. Given remedial treatment his IQ may show an increase. Whether or not some permanency of damage may be expected is argued both ways. The teacher's obligation is to recognize the needs of the culturally deprived child, connect him with essential experiences, and carry him educationally forward as far as possible.

Research in the field of mental retardation. Research in the field of mental retardation is constantly in progress. What is the prevalence of mental retardation? What are the causes? What are the treatments? What are the sociological implications of mental retardation? What educational procedures should be employed? Many studies have been made that are worthy of being called scientific research. In other cases conclusions have been drawn from inadequate or poorly controlled observations and procedures. The general use of statistical methods in the field of research is adding to the permanency of findings. Moreover, the study of mental retardation is no longer in the hands of a few. More and more time is being devoted to its study by more and more people, and it is the increased practice to combine and refine pooled knowledges.

The scope of this chapter. Volumes have been written about the types, causes, and treatments of mental retardation, and new knowledges are being constantly added. What is said in this chapter is not offered as a substitute for study in the field. It is only intended to open up the field and briefly indicate to the teacher the need for further study. It is intended to alert him* to the need for evaluating materials read gauged by the probable reliability of the research involved. It is intended to direct his attention to the need for interpreting what he reads in terms of the needs of his pupils individually and collectively.

SUGGESTED READINGS

SARASON, SEYMOUR B.: Psychological Problems in Mental Deficiency, 3rd ed. New York, Harper and Brothers, 1953.

This book should help the teacher understand the nature of mental retardation. It indicates the complexity of the problem. It discusses the criteria of identification and the forms and treatments of mental retardation. It freely quotes and presents the viewpoints of authorities in the field.

CRUICKSHANK, WILLIAM M., and others: A Teaching Method for Brain-Injured and Hyperactive Children. Syracuse, Syracuse University Press, 1961.

This book should be helpful to the teacher whose class includes one or more children who have been classified as brain-injured or who are unduly hyperactive—the children who fail to respond to ordinarily successful educational and corrective methods.

GARTON, MALINDA DEAN: Teaching the Educable Mentally Retarded. Chapter 2. Characteristics of the Educable Mentally Retarded. Springfield, Ill., Charles C Thomas, 1961.

A good summary of the predominant characteristics and traits of the educable mentally retarded.

---

* Designation of the teacher is made by means of masculine pronouns in this text.

2/

Qualifications for a Teacher
of the Mentally Retarded

General qualifications for a teacher of the educable mentally retarded. The teacher of the educable mentally retarded should possess the skills, qualifications and strength of character expected of a well qualified teacher of the primary or elementary school grades. He should receive specific instruction in the psychological, sociological, and educational implications of mental retardation so that he may understand the needs of the retarded, and the procedures to be followed in meeting these needs.

The teacher of the mentally retarded should have a basic educational philosophy. The teacher should be guided by an educational philosophy founded on an understanding of the mentally retarded and their needs, and the principles involved in the fulfillment of those needs. He should be able to choose teaching materials on the basis of their relative merits as measured by their influence upon the growth and development of a child. He should be able to judge the comparative values of different teaching methods and select those most likely to bring desired results. The teacher should be able to evaluate

6

success as measured by the progress shown by pupils. He should know why he is teaching what he is teaching. *The teacher of the mentally retarded should be possessed of the following traits:*

1. MATURITY AND STABILITY. The full acceptance of the responsibilities demanded of a teacher of the mentally retarded requires maturity. The person who lacks self discipline cannot be expected to develop that quality in children of limited intellectual abilities.

2. HEALTH AND VIGOR. Classroom duties are strenuous. Aside from regular classroom duties there will be a need to perform many extracurricular duties which activate and give vitality to teaching. The teacher should not be so fatigued by professional activities that there is no opportunity to "live a life of his own."

3. PATIENCE AND TOLERANCE. Patience is required to teach the child who comprehends feebly, learns slowly and forgets easily. A higher than average number of mental retardates deviate from the normal in physical appearance, or are hampered by coordination defects. Any aversion on the part of the teacher toward some physical anomaly is likely to be sensed by the child no matter how well the teacher attempts to conceal it.

4. CHEERFULNESS. Cheerfulness is an important asset for the retardate, and he readily emulates the moods of his teacher.

5. CALMNESS. The excitable, overly demonstrative teacher overstimulates his pupils and creates behavior problems.

6. ADAPTABILITY. The teacher of the mentally retarded deals with a variety of personalities with varying needs. He deals with varied and inconstant situations. Teaching success depends largely upon the ability to adjust teaching procedures as pupil needs and situations direct.

7. RESOURCEFULNESS. The teacher of the mentally retarded often needs to seek out materials of instruction not pro-

vided for in the school set-up. He can often profit from the advice and help of individuals in the community. The teacher needs to be able to recognize resources as resources.

8. ORIGINALITY. When interest lags the teacher should be able to devise new and different ways of presenting materials so as to recapture lost interest. The teacher who is required to follow a prearranged curriculum will need to devise means of vitalizing and adapting it to fit more nearly the needs and interests of the pupils subjected to it.

9. A COOPERATIVE ATTITUDE. The teacher of the mentally retarded may be called upon to cooperate with individuals who can furnish psychological, medical or sociological information about pupils. He will be called upon to cooperate with other educators—the supervisor, the principal, and fellow teachers. The more cooperatively the teacher reacts toward them, the more help he can expect from them.

10. DESIRE FOR KNOWLEDGE. In order to better understand his pupils and interpret the advice furnished by specialists, the teacher needs to keep abreast of new developments concerning studies, experimentations, and findings relating to mental retardation.

The teacher of the mentally retarded should recognize the benefits of allied efforts. The teacher should be ready and willing to become allied with such educational, parental, and sociological organizations as may be beneficial to him as an educator of the mentally retarded. Teaching strength may be found in the exchange of information and ideas, or research projects may be shared. Of course, a teacher cannot join every organization of professional worth, but there should be an awareness of the benefits to be derived from cooperative efforts, and membership maintained in some carefully chosen few.

No teacher will be a model of perfection. Certainly no teacher will deserve placement at the top of each quality listed as desirable for a teacher of the mentally retarded. The indicated qualifications should serve to point out, to the teacher or prospective teacher, individual strengths and weaknesses, and should indicate the directions efforts toward improvement should take.

If a scale were devised to measure the qualities discussed, the individual teaching, or preparing to teach, the educable mentally retarded should score above the median.

3/

Principles Underlying the Education of the Mentally Retarded

The general objective in the training of the mentally retarded. The general objective in the education of any retardate should be to prepare him to live what is for him the "good life"—a life lived as happily, actively, and purposively as potentialities permit. The nature and scope of the curriculum should consider his interests and his mental and social capacities as related to the opportunities which his area of living may be expected to afford him.

The special classroom should be a laboratory for child study. If best results are to be obtained, the special class teacher will need to be a clinically-minded individual. The teacher should by nature and training be able to look at each child as an integral human whole. Although he should be well aware of the child's limitations there should be even more awareness of his possibilities. The teacher should have knowledge of how to uncover a child's hidden talents and special aptitudes. He needs to have a broad understanding of how to inter-

10

pret child behavior as related to inherent and environmental factors and influences. The child may need to be observed and studied for some time before the best answers to his problems may be found.

The best placement for a mentally retarded child is with a group of his peers. The best school placement for a mentally retarded child is with a group of children whose interests and capacities to learn are comparable, within reasonable limitations, to his own capacity. The more homogeneous the group is in terms of mental age, chronological age, and social achievement, the better are the learning opportunities individually and collectively. However, even in a special class where the range of ages is fairly wide, the retardate will usually feel more at home, and accomplish more, than he will in a regular classroom where he is noticeably oversized physically and undersized academically.

The nature and scope of the curriculum should be in accordance with the mental capacity of the child. This axiom as applied to curricular choices for the mental retardate means that much that is included in the curricula of mentally normal children should be deleted, or curtailed and simplified. It means the addition of things of importance that are learned by the average child through casual contact, but which may go unlearned by the retarded child unless he is specifically taught.

The curriculum should not be limited to a series of texts, topics or divisions of instruction. The curriculum should be thought of as embodying a mass of habits and attitudes. The retardate's ability to acquire habits of good conduct is often less limited than his ability to learn the common school subjects. Good behavior can be taught to a large percentage of mentally retarded children. The retardate's success in life is often more influenced by the habits and attitudes he acquires than by his stock of informations and skills, important as some of them are. Experience has shown that the retarded employee, who is punctual and diligent, may have more security on his job than the one who can read more fluently but does not punch the time clock with punctuality or lacks interest in his work. The slow-minded fellow with a good-natured disposition may get along with less trouble than does the ill-natured man of greater intelligence who cannot live at peace with his neighbors. *The selection of curricular material should be determined by its usefulness.* Since time is short and the retardate's pace is slow, those things which are relatively more practically, socially, or morally useful to the retardate deserve first curricular consideration. The time and effort required to learn something should be weighed against the value of its learning. It is granted that many worthwhile learnings are more intangible than tangible, and the teacher's good judgment may be the only scale for their measurement.

The mentally retarded child needs firsthand experiences. The mentally retarded child is not to any extent a vicarious learner. He learns through firsthand experiences. For example, while pictures will often facilitate learning, the ones which depict things the child has already met in real life will have more meaning for him. A picture of an old woman in a family setting may not represent "grandmother" to him unless he has had intimate contact with a grandmother of his own. Until he has visited a farm, pictures of farm scenes will not be the best departures for learning in the area of language and reading. Unless he has watched a lion pacing in his cage and heard him roaring at the zoo, or has seen him performing in a circus, he will have little idea of what a lion is really like. The retarded child needs more reinforcement of his learnings by actual contacts and experiences than does a child of normal intelligence.

The mentally retarded child should be taught functionally. The mentally retarded child is slow to see relationships between things. He is slow in learning to transfer knowledges acquired in one situation to others where they might apply. He is slow in learning to make generalizations. It is important that what he is taught in school be taught in real life situations or situations approximating those he will meet in real life.

Instruction should not begin too early. It is unwise to try to teach a mentally retarded child something before he is mentally old enough to learn it. An attitude of distaste may be built up which will interfere with learning when sufficient mental maturity has been reached. It is a waste of time and effort to try to teach a child things he is not mentally equipped to learn. *Teaching should begin at the pupil's level.* The teacher should begin at the child's level in experiences, knowledges and skills, at his mental, educational and emotional level. The point of departure should be sufficiently low, while the ultimate goal should be the highest that is significantly useful to the individual. *Much repetition is needed.* Most facts and ways of doing things need to be brought again and again to the attention of the mentally retarded child before they become his own. On occasion, something may be so forcibly or uniquely brought to the attention of the child that he does not forget it, but most of his learning will be acquired through meaningful repetitive contacts and repeated practice. He needs to encounter most facts of learning more frequently than does the average child before he can firmly implant them in his memory.

All applicable sensory approaches possible should be utilized in the teaching of the mentally retarded child. The more inroads from the outer to the inner world of the mentally retarded child that can be utilized to direct his experiences, the broader will be his learning. Learning is facilitated and quickened by the utilization of all sensory avenues that naturally apply to a situation. If a mentally retarded child can hear, touch, and smell as well as see something, that something will have more meaning for him.

Abstract meanings are difficult for the mental retardate to understand. The mental retardate thinks more concretely than he does abstractly. He needs to be taught as concretely and specifically as possible. Before he can be taught the meaning of the word "sanitation," he must be taught specifically to wash

dishes properly, to keep the lid on the garbage pail, etc. He
learns the meaning of honesty through its application to specific situations. However, he should be helped to understand
qualities apart from the situations in which he learns them as
well as he can.

The vividness of stimuli should be increased. While the
schoolroom cannot be expected to afford a round of spectacular
events, effort should be made to present facts of learning as
vividly as is reasonably possible. To watch a butterfly emerge
from a cocoon will leave its impression, whereas pages of nature
study that are read may be quickly forgotten. Bargaining over
the counter of a play store is a quicker way of learning how to
make change than is dependence upon drill in problems of
subtraction.

The implanting of fallacious ideas should be avoided. The
implantation of a wrong idea is illustrated by the story of the
young retarded pupil who, when asked to solve a simple problem in addition involving children, said, "Those numbers are
for apples." His experience in addition had been with apples
which his teacher had used to teach numbers. A mentally
retarded girl was confused when she began to use the letters
of the alphabet for spelling. At home she had learned by heart
the contents of an ABC book. Many of the letters were so
closely associated in her mind with the words for which they
stood that she frequently substituted the word for the letter.
For example, she usually spelled her name, Ann, "Apple-n-n."

Multiple contacts should be provided. The way to avoid
the implantation of wrong ideas is to provide opportunities for
responding in more than one situation. The way for a child to
learn a fact that applies to, or in, more than one situation is
by applying and using it in different situations. To learn to
read a word well enough so that he recognizes it every time
he sees it requires that provision be made for him to encounter
it in different reading contexts. He is more likely to remember
how to spell a word if he meets it in his reading, studies it from

his spelling list, writes it in his composition and uses it in a letter to a friend.

Discouragement should be avoided. Tasks assigned should be difficult enough to offer some challenge, but easy enough so that opportunities for discouragement are minimized. Praise should be freely used. Whenever possible, success should be tangible to the pupil himself; it should not always be necessary for a child's teacher to tell him he has succeeded. It is better when a child's recognition of accomplishment precedes his teacher's praise of it, but the added incentive to further effort should not be omitted.

Interest should be kept at a high level. The task the child approaches willingly is usually the one he learns more readily. The greater his degree of interest, the more facile his learning. His natural interests should be preserved and nurtured to the fullest extent that is compatible with growth and development. When interest lags in the learning of facts and skills of importance, new teaching approaches should be used to recapture the interests of the child.

4/

Use of Tests by the Classroom Teacher

A psychological examination should be a requirement for assignment to a class for mentally retarded children. The examination should include the application of a well-standardized individual intelligence test as, for example, the widely used Terman-Merrill revision of the Stanford-Binet tests.

Results of the psychological examination should be made available to the classroom teacher. The teacher should be furnished a summary of the examination results, together with any suggestions the psychologist may believe to be helpful. The summary should state the examinee's IQ and his M.A. (mental age) at the date of examination. The teacher should be informed of the results of other tests—additional verbal tests, performance tests, motor tests, tests of social intelligence, and the like. Any information about previous school experiences, known behavior peculiarities, cultural backgrounds, etc., should be passed on to the teacher. If, as is highly desirable, a medical examination has been included in the child's clinical examination, the teacher should be informed of any findings which may help him understand the child or influence teaching procedures.

The use of group intelligence tests in the special classroom.
Assuming that pupils have been properly assigned and that
the teacher has been furnished with a summary of individual
test results, there is little need for the use of group intelligence
tests in a class for mentally retarded children. There is no
teaching advantage to be gained from the comparative ratings
that such tests would furnish the teacher. Primarily the child
should be placed in competition with himself. Only in areas
where he is well equipped to compete as gauged not only by
mental ability, but also by previous attainments, should the
mentally retarded child be asked to compete with others. Competition is mentally healthful only if the individual is equipped
to compete. Assuming pupils have been individually tested,
the use of group tests offers no teaching advantages. There may
be situations where group testing is justified as a part of a
school survey or in connection with some research project.

*Should the teacher of a special class give individual intelli-
gence tests?* It is seldom that a classroom teacher has the
qualifications necessary for administering individual intelligence tests. Most teachers lack the training and experience
needed to qualify them. A general course in testing or the
reading and use of a manual is not adequate preparation. There
are many excellent teachers who are poor testers. Some unwit-
tingly invalidate test results because, by nature, they cannot
refrain from teaching as they test—to give a hint, or ask a
provocative question. In many places, and that is as it should
be, children may not be assigned to special classes unless ex-
amined by a certified tester or a licensed psychologist.

Retests. Retests should be given from time to time to establish beyond a reasonable doubt the validity of the diagnosis
upon which a child's entrance into a class for retarded children
was based. Even though the IQ obtained on a test given by a
qualified tester is a generally reliable measure, there are factors
over which the examiner has no control, but which may occasionally influence the validity of the IQ. Unless there are significant reasons why an early retest is indicated as desirable, a re-

test after a child has been in a special class a year or so is a good rule to follow. If there is no appreciable change in IQ, another test a year or so before the child is scheduled to leave school is a wise procedure. Children with fluctuating IQ's should be tested annually until, and if, the IQ remains reasonably constant.

Teacher responsibility for retests. It is recognized that lack of personnel makes the above suggestions administratively impossible in many school situations. It is also recognized that the teacher is not ordinarily responsible for testing programs or rules of referral, but when a pupil's performance does not coincide with what his mental age indicates might be expected, the teacher may need to report observations to the proper supervisory agency. If a pupil is performing well beyond the expectancy of his mental age the need for an immediate retest is clearly indicated, particularly if the discrepancy is so wide that the wisdom of his placement may be in question. If the discrepancy is on the minus side, and before a retest is recommended, it is suggested that the pupil be observed and studied to determine if his low performance may be explained by physical, environmental, or emotional interferences.

Discrepancies between performances and mental levels indicate a need for investigation and study. After allowances have been made for educational deficiencies that are the result of lack of training or faulty training and if a pupil's rate of progress is not commensurate (within reasonable limitations) with that which his IQ indicates it should be, the pupil should be made the subject of observation and study to locate the cause of learning difficulties. After the teacher has searched for conditions of health, presence of physical defects, and damaging environmental and emotional influences that may be obstructing school progress, and has been able to uncover the probable deterrents to progress, he should make such adjustments as are believed may better conditions. The severity or specialized nature of conditions may indicate the need for referral of the case to someone specially equipped to find the cause and suggest or apply remedial measures. If the teacher's best efforts to narrow the gap between capacity to learn and actual learning fail, he should seek the best available help. He should, of course, first make use of sources of help within the school system.

The choice of group achievement tests. The value of the use of standardized achievement tests with educable retarded pupils depends upon the carefulness with which they are chosen. The test that puts a premium on speed is to be avoided. The content and difficulty of a test should be selected to fit a pupil's level of probable attainment. While it may extend some beyond his level of attainment, the test should contain only a relatively small percentage of problems which the pupil is unable to solve.

What achievement tests are most suitable? Tests, chiefly at the primary level, in reading and arithmetic are probably the most useful standardized tests to be used with retarded pupils. Standardized arithmetic tests at the intermediate level are apt to include arithmetical facts and problems that have been deleted from the curriculum of the retarded pupil. Standardized tests of informational subjects usually include much material which the retarded pupil has had no opportunity to study. The teacher, in making tests to fit the curricular needs of pupils, can gain insight into methods of questioning and testing by studying standardized tests. Of course results obtained cannot be compared with the norms of the test from which materials or ideas may have been borrowed.

Making use of standardized achievement test results. If a child has been exposed to reading and arithmetic before entrance into a special class, the early application of standardized tests in these subjects will help the teacher to know where to start in his teaching. Testing from time to time will indicate the progress made in the tested areas. A pupil's progress should be judged more by the amount of learning during a given period than by comparison to norms for the child's age. Is his rate of progress in proportion to what his IQ indicates it should be? Manuals for use with certain standardized tests often give valuable suggestions for detecting individual needs, and sometimes indicate remedial procedures.

The use of teacher-made tests. The slavish dependence upon tests is apt to result in mechanical teaching and is apt to distract the teacher's attention from important goals in teaching, but the conservative use of well-planned tests with educable retardates serves a purpose. They can point out to the teacher and pupil that certain facts have or have not been learned. If tests are not too difficult, so that the pupil may attain a fair measure of success, they may provide for the examinee a feeling of kinship with regular grade pupils who are subjected to regular testing. This may be particularly true if testing periods in the special class are planned to coincide with testing periods of regular grade pupils of corresponding chronological ages. To receive a grade of say 90, or whatever represents a good grade to his schoolmates in the regular grades, may make the retardate proud of his achievements, and may serve as an incentive to further learning.

What constitutes a good test? A good test for the mentally retarded pupil is one that includes facts that are really worth his knowing, and to which the child has had some learning exposure. Catch questions have no place in tests for retardates, nor do questions of an abstract nature. Tests should be short so that the child's attention span is not overtaxed. Unless reading is being tested, reading requirements should be held to a minimum.

Tests should be graduated in difficulty. Tests should not be so easy that they present no challenge to those tested, but neither should they be so difficult that a large percentage of failures result. If the nature of the test permits, it should contain problems of graduated difficulty. It may contain some important facts of review as well as recently studied materials. The results should indicate what facts need further study and furnish some clues to whether or not sufficient repetition is being employed. An overabundance of failures indicates the need to slow down; perfection or near perfection indicates that less time and study may be required for the acquisition of certain facts.

Tests should be chosen to fit individual needs. Tests should be given only to those for whom they have testing value. If a group testing period is used, enough different tests should be prepared to cover individual needs. Sometimes not more than one or two pupils will be taking a particular test.

SUGGESTED READING

BROWNELL, WILLIAM A.: The Measurement of Understanding (Nat'l. Soc. for Study of Education, 45th yearbook, part I). Chicago, University of Chicago Press, 1946.

The teacher, who has had no training in the use of tests and who lacks supervisory assistance in the selection of proper testing materials, may find some help in this comprehensive, well-prepared report. It may clarify the general purposes of testing. Discrimination in locating and selecting the information that will be most useful to a teacher of the mentally retarded will be needed.

5/

Grouping and Programing
in the Special Class

The teacher's responsibility for the use of time. The teacher
of the special class has much more freedom of choice in planning programs than does the average teacher, but along with
this freedom goes increased responsibility for results obtained.
The best check on the wisdom of program choices and time al-
lotments is a frequent inventory of each child's progress in
terms of knowledges and skills gained and habits and attitudes
acquired. The ideal classroom situation would be one where
every minute of the school day the pupil is growing and developing.

Need for group participation. Each and every child in a
special class for retarded children will require considerable
individual attention, but he should also experience some group
participation. Learning to work and play with others is a
necessary part of his social development and also widens his
scope of possible learnings. Groupings based on homogeneity
of needs and interests are great time savers, and there is never
enough classroom time to teach retardates as many things as
they might be able to learn.

Group placements. There are some situations such as opening exercises and game and recreational periods where the

class as a whole may perform as a group. A pupil's placement in smaller classroom groups should be based on his chances of learning within those groups. Though there is a natural relationship between success and mental ages and IQ's, achievements and social needs should determine group placements. A pupil may not fit in with any one group for all subjects and activities. He may profitably perform part of the time with one group and part of the time with another. He should be placed in whichever group offers him the best chance for improvement and success in the subject or activity involved. A pupil with a relatively low IQ will often work quite willingly with children somewhat lower in chronological age if no one calls attention to the fact that he is the oldest and biggest one in the group; however, if he shows signs of self-consciousness because of his size he should be removed from the group even if it means establishing a class of one.

Definite time periods. The retardate should learn that a regard for time appointments and schedules is a part of practical living. If he is to acquire the habit of being on time, opportunities for adhering to certain time demands should be provided. The daily program should include some regularly timed activities. As far as possible the pupil should assume responsibility for observance of these time schedules. Being on time for school is the first step toward acquisition of the habit. Other time-defined periods may be the midsession lunch period, recess periods, or some time-scheduled activity with regular grade pupils, as gymnastics or manual arts. If a time schedule is violated, it should be for an important reason, and the pupil should be made aware of the reason.

Time blocks. Rather than preparing a program with a number of short periods and listing the exact time each group is to be instructed, time spent in program preparation will be lessened and individual needs better met if a block of time is assigned to a subject being taught to a number of groups of varying levels of achievement. For example, if four reading groups are required, a block of time sufficient to cover all four groups may be placed on the program, rather than allotting a

certain number of minutes of instructional time to each group
and listing the times of their meetings. This allows more lee-
way in shortening or lengthening periods as needed from day
to day. The period for any one group is considered ended when
a natural, rather than a time-dictated, stopping point has been
reached.

Comparative needs should be considered. The first consideration in apportioning time to different subjects and activities should be the needs of individual pupils. The most imperative needs for any child at any time should be used to gauge
the amount of time devoted to the study of any subject or the
amount spent with any activity or project. The length of a time
block in the daily program for any one subject should be determined by the number of participating groups and the amount
of time needed for the successful completion of tasks.

Some specific suggestions. The child who has not attained
above a first grade level of reading should have not less than
two definite instructional periods in reading each day. It has
been demonstrated that a number of shorter periods have a
better effect upon learning than one or two long periods. After
a child is reading well at a second grade level, one daily formal
instructional period (well supplemented by reading incidental
to other activities) plus a period devoted to word analysis will
ordinarily be sufficient unless the child's reading achievement
age is below his mental age. The amount of time devoted to
spelling should be determined by spelling needs; if the pupil is
well supplied with word reference lists to prevent error in his
written work, a formal period every other day should be sufficient. These formal periods should be supplemented by practice in the writing of words needed in written composition. The
teaching of writing should be closely allied to the practical
situations where writing is needed. Definite periods for the
teaching of writing should be discontinued as soon as a child
can write with a reasonable degree of legibility and ease. The
amount of time devoted to the study of arithmetic should be
determined by the pupil's apparent needs. The awkward,

poorly coordinated child needs to devote more time to physical training than does the one who seems to get along as well as do most of the children with whom he plays. The amount of time devoted to games and recreational activities should be measured by the usefulness of the activities involved in terms of physical and social betterment.

Rotation periods. The wider the ranges of IQ's and chronological ages within a class, the more individualized instruction becomes. The larger the number of instructional groups, the more instructional time is consumed. It takes retarded children longer than children of normal intelligence to become orientated when they change from one classroom situation to another. They do not quickly center their thoughts on a new situation. These time-consuming factors make daily programing difficult. When there is a wide range of abilities represented within a class it may be found advantageous to use a system of program rotation. Certain subjects taught one day may be omitted the next day, but the order of the appearance of the subjects in the program remains unchanged. In making such a program the teacher may leave certain blocks in the program marked *Rotation Subjects.* Each of the subjects, together with the groups of students studying it, is listed on a separate card so that the cards may be rotated. Certain subjects are not included in the rotated list, but are taught daily or on certain days of the week. Reading is one of the subjects which should be taught daily. Also there should be daily opportunity for development in language usage, including a chance for every child to express himself verbally at some time during the day. Certain major projects deserve daily attention.

Planning unsupervised time. The larger proportion of a pupil's school day is spent without the direct supervision of his teacher. Of course the teacher has to be a many-eyed, many-eared creature who knows what is going on most of the time. He needs to be able to readily spot the unoccupied or poorly-occupied pupil and be ready to suggest to him what to do, while at the same time carrying on the task of immediate concern. The things the pupil does during the time he is not working directly under teacher-supervision should have educational worth. They should be furthering his training in some academic, practical, social or ethical way. To prevent waste, idleness and mischief, there is need for planning.

Conserving the teacher's time. There are many materials available commercially which, if chosen with individual pupils in mind, are valuable teaching aids and cut down the amount of time used in the preparation of materials. Included are color and word and number teaching devices, reading-readiness seat materials, reading and arithmetic teaching devices, map puzzles, etc. A duplicating machine of some sort may be used to prevent repetitious preparation. Pupils should be trained to know where to find things and what to do next, without always having to consult the teacher. When assignments have been completed, there should be other occupations readily available. A certain amount of choice should be permitted pupils in the selection of things to do. It is sometimes desirable for the teacher, or better still the pupil if he can, to make memos of things to be done and the order in which they should be done.

Suggestions for the planning of the pupil's time:

Young retardates should have play materials readily accessible to turn to when they are not otherwise occupied. A child may wish to play by himself or seek the companionship of others in some type of play activity. The completion of previously assigned tasks, refraining from becoming disorderly or noisy, and reasonable care in the handling of materials should be the only restrictions placed upon his play activities.

Seatwork assignments which supplement class procedures should be freely used. A pre-class period may make use of materials of preparation for the period, or a post-class period may be used to give further practice in facts and knowledges presented or be used to check on the learnings of the period.

Practice materials may often be filed in a way so that items needing practice or review are made readily accessible. Word and dictionary files should be readily available for the pupil's use in his reading or writing. Word files and pupil-made dictionaries should vary in the nature of their make-up according to the levels of learning of those they are designed to serve. The pupil should be taught to use word lists and dictionaries to avoid and correct errors as independently as he can.

Group projects may be turned to individually, or cooperatively with one or two other classmates who also have no priority assignments, for work on uncompleted tasks connected with the project. When there is a group conference regarding some classroom project under way, tasks which may be individually worked upon during otherwise unoccupied moments may be pointed out and ways and means discussed.

Pupils may have individual projects in the making which may be carried on with a minimal amount of supervision—a piece of handwork, a notebook or a hobby pursuit. Pupils may sometimes spend time profitably hunting for articles, books, information, illustrations or materials related to an activity in progress. Many concomitant learnings may result from such searching. Search may contribute to the completion of an individual or group project. The field of the pupil's search should be comparatively narrow, and the directions given should be explicit so that some measure of success in his findings may be assured.

The discretionary use of pupils as teachers of each other has its merits. With the aid of number combination cards, which have the combination and its answer on one side and only the combination on the other, pupils may check each other. The combinations needing drill may be laid aside, and taken to his seat by the pupil needing practice and used as a guide for self-practice techniques. Pupils may dictate and correct the spelling lists of each other. The pupil needing practice in easy reading may be permitted to read to younger children. The pupil who can make change correctly (at least as far as certain amounts are involved) may act as storekeeper or cashier, helping customers with their change-making problems. The pupil who has attained certain manual or physical skills may help others who would like to attain these same skills. Of course, pupils should be used for teaching purposes only when, and if, their instructional services are willingly accepted.

Activity units in the program. There should be a time set aside in the program when the teacher will discuss plans with pupils and offer such advice and directions as are necessary to further the progress of activity units with which they may be employed. Sometimes the successful completion of a project may naturally define time limits, while in other cases the amount of time spent may be increased or decreased as deemed advisable. Usually a project will furnish incentives and materials for learning in correlated subjects. The work involved may be accomplished as an integral part of the project itself, or the study involved in certain correlated subjects may be transferred to the times allotted in the program for these subjects, and either period lengthened or shortened if there is need. The amount of time allowed for an activity unit will advisedly depend upon the worthwhileness of learnings involved in terms of knowledges or skills gained and the habits and attitudes acquired by participants in the project.

Excursions. The program should be flexible enough to permit fairly frequent excursions by the class. Excursions should be planned with learning results in mind. An excursion may be a pleasant temporary experience or one that opens up avenues of worthwhile learning. The same excursion may provide opportunities of learning for different levels of abilities. An excursion in connection with a social studies project being carried on by older pupils may also furnish younger pupils with materials for conversation, language development, and self-experience reading stories. Walks taken about the school neighborhood may be used to help pupils better orient themselves. They may learn rules of polite and safe conduct, to read significant signs, locations of places of interest and usefulness, how to locate places from given addresses, and the like. Neighborhood excursions may be used to introduce older students to the practical use of maps. There should be beforehand discussions to prepare pupils to get the most out of excursions, and some of the things observed should be incorporated in follow-up classroom learning situations.

Group versus individual needs. Although on the whole the usage of time should be with the individual in mind, there are certain situations where all the children in the room participate in some group activity. One of the main objectives of such performances is to teach the child that he is not just a person unto himself but is also a member of society, and to learn that self-interests must sometimes be sacrificed for group interests. In such a classroom situation the needs of the group should be given preference over individual needs, and one pupil should not be permitted to demand time and attention for himself to the neglect of the group as a whole. Group situations may often be used to build up respect for individual talents and attainments.

The program should be a tentative arrangement. The success of a program lies with the ability of the teacher to recognize the instructional needs of the pupils, the ability to evaluate the results of teaching, and the ability to make changes as their need is indicated. The program is therefore always in a tentative state. Its validity can be measured only by the growth and development of pupils.

6/

Considering the Individual Needs of the Mentally Retarded School Child

Getting to know the pupil and his needs. The initial duty of the teacher of mentally retarded children is to gather as complete knowledge as possible about each child—his inherent intellectual possibilities; his medical and health background; his family background and ways of living; his neighborhood surroundings; his previous school experiences and attainments; his use of leisure time; skills, knowledges, habits and attitudes acquired to date; and the degree of acceptance or non-acceptance by family members, neighbors, and school associates. Not all these things will be learned at one time, but as much as is possible of the general picture should be gathered as soon as possible. His learning needs bear direct relationship to all of this information.

The beginning days of school. The first few days of school the teacher will be occupied with probing and informal testing to find out what knowledges, skills, habits and attitudes each pupil has already acquired. In order that the pupil may not immediately experience failure, the teacher should start testing with tasks the child can reasonably be expected to perform successfully. Increasingly difficult tasks may be assigned until a satisfactory point of departure for further teaching has been reached. For the first few days of school, until newcomers have had a chance to find out that school may be a pleasant place in which to live, more than an ordinary amount of time may need to be spent with story-telling, games, and recreational or handwork activities. The program should be allowed to fall into its normal pattern as soon as is feasible. Although after a vacation period a certain amount of review will be necessary, a former member of the class will usually require less preliminary probing than does the child just beginning his school career or one coming as a transfer from another schoolroom situation.

Cumulative records. A folder to hold temporary and permanent records should be provided for each pupil. Informational data that accompanied the child's entrance into the special class, past school records and a summary of the psychological findings upon which his entrance into the class was based, should be included among the records. Accounts of home visitations, observations on home and neighborhood conditions, and parental responses to home visits should be recorded. All information that will keep the child before the eyes of the teacher as an individual with specific potentialities and needs should be included. The teacher cannot carry in mind all the details that may have import for the child's growth and development. Entries should be dated so that progress, or the lack of it, may be noted.

Records of school progress should be included. Samples of written work, arithmetic papers, lists of books read, etc., are often definite teaching aids. Records may provide the means for observing step-by-step progress and indicate rates of progress. At the end of the school year some of the samples saved during the year may be eliminated, and certain reports may be summarized, but enough should be retained to clearly indicate what progress has been made during the school year.

The cumulative record should be carried on from year to year, and should be sent to the next teacher when a transfer is made. Thoughtfully prepared records furnish the teacher with materials for evaluating his successes and failures. The cumulative record furnishes information to supervisors and principals who are unable to follow the day-by-day progress of each child.

Recordings should be stated in specific terms. Recordings should be as specifically stated as possible. To record that a pupil has made progress in his social development is a vaguely useful statement, but one to the effect that he shows no inclination to play with other children and a later statement that for the first time he voluntarily joined a group of children at play have meaning. The teacher who is striving to help a pupil make better social adjustments needs to know something about his specific maladjustments. To say that a pupil is slow in arithmetic is no help at all to the teacher who wants to know what the child needs to be taught, whereas an arithmetic paper showing up specific errors indicates what steps should be taken next. A later sample may indicate mastery over these previously unlearned number facts. Dated samples of arithmetic papers and other types of written work may be valuable indicators of learning needs and progress made in the subjects represented. A list of readers and other books read should be kept. Any notable accomplishment in any phase of school work and any newly acquired habit or attitude should be recorded.

Memoranda sheets. The teacher cannot afford to take the time to record accurately every matter of importance, each and every item of significance, as they immediately come to notice. However, memories are too fallible to be relied upon to recall all of these things at some later date. It is suggested that the teacher keep a memo pad or sheet on which reminders and notations may be hastily jotted down to be more permanently recorded at a later time. A single word or two, together with a child's name, may be sufficient to jog the memory, and whatever deserves permanent recording may be entered in more accurate form in the child's cumulative record at a convenient time.

Take time to look at the child as an individual. Many teachers, who are quite adept at measuring a pupil's academic needs and progress, are less adept at appraising his personality and social needs. The teacher needs to take time to think of the child as a person with individual abilities and needs, an integral human whole. The teacher needs to look at him as he is today, and anticipate what he may be expected to be tomorrow. Is what he is doing and learning adding to his maturity? It is suggested that when a teacher is making entries in cumulative records is a good time to give thought to the child as a particular child with peculiar needs and outlooks.

Individual talents and interests should be encouraged. If some special interest may be found, something in which a child is relatively more capable, or at least relatively more interested, than most of his classmates, it may be made to serve him as a personality builder. It has special value if it is something that may be observed by others and win favorable comment. As any other child, the mentally retarded one likes to do some things by himself, to express himself as a distinct personality. Perhaps he has a good singing voice and likes to use it. He may be permitted to join some regular grade class during its music hour. At least he should have a chance to sing. Perhaps he can learn to play a harmonica. An occasional mental retardate will be found who shows considerable ability in copying pictures made by more creative artists. He has, what is for him, a valuable talent. The child who is especially adept at any type of handicraft has a talent worth encouraging. A child with a foreign background may be able to perform a native dance of the country from which his parents came; let him dance sometimes. Another child may have some hobby interest; give him a chance to display the results of his talent to others.

A special period for the display of talents may be provided. It is suggested that a period once a week be set aside to give pupils an opportunity to perform before or exhibit something to an audience comprised of the remainder of the class, a visitor or two from the other grades, or a parent or friend from outside the school. Each child should at some time have an opportunity to appear or have his talents in some way exhibited on the program. Some will need more help in preparation than others. The child who is overly reluctant to appear before an audience may be helped to believe that his work or activity is worthy of exhibition if the teacher, with words of commendation, displays a piece of handicraft made by the child or reads a story written by him. Perhaps the child has a hobby of collecting things, and as the child holds up objects before the eyes of the spectators, the teacher may make explanatory remarks. The teacher, while speaking, may pause to ask the child a question or two regarding his project, thus easing him into a talking situation. If the child loses his self-consciousness sufficiently, he may be encouraged to add his own explanatory remarks. Self-activities should be encouraged; self-expression is a part of the maturing process.

Social guidance of the individual mental retardate. Every mentally retarded child needs more social guidance than a teacher is equipped or has the time to give him. If home guidance is inadequate or if a child has some specific needs which neither home nor school is able to satisfy, an outside source should be sought to help with the problem. That source may be an organized social agency, a leader of a youth or recreational group, the pastor or a person suggested by the pastor of the church which the child's family attends, a prospective employer, or an individual willing and capable of acting as a big brother or sister of the retardate. Sometimes merely finding the suitable play or recreational group for a retardate may put him in a position to find companionship of the right sort, solving an existent social need. Placing the retarded pupil in music, physical education, industrial arts, or other regular grade class —chosen because it is believed that there he has a chance to attain at least average success—is often a good social guidance measure.

A fourteen year old boy was an attendant in the upper group of a special class center. Both his father and his mother were employed, and there was little parental supervision. The boy became acquainted with a couple of boys from a nearby Junior High School who were well known for their undisciplined behavior. He met these boys every night after school and received instruction from them in ways of destroying property, annoying people, and committing petty thievery.

The custodian of the school which the fourteen year old attended noted what was happening to the boy and reported his observations to the school principal. The principal and the custodian worked out a plan to keep the boy occupied so that he would have neither time nor need to seek the company of his erstwhile "friends." He was given an after-school job as the custodian's assistant, a small salary for this work being obtained from funds available to the principal for welfare work. The custodian frequently took the boy home with him for a snack, or for supper. A lasting friendship grew between the custodian and his helper. Even after the young man was out of school and had found employment, he continued to bring his problems to the custodian for discussion and advice.

Independence of action. The mentally retarded child should be encouraged to act as independently as he prudently and considerately can. He should, as far as he is capable, learn the meaning of self-direction. He should take charge of his own activities to the full extent that self-interest and group-interest permit. He should take as much responsibility as he is able for knowing when to leave one activity and start another. If he has completed an assignment and if it is not yet time for his next time-allotted task, he should have other tasks or activities to which he may turn without consulting his teacher. He should not, however, be permitted to flit from one thing to another without regard to accomplishment. He should be taught that when he moves about the room it should be for a purpose, and at a time and in a manner that does not distract the attention of others at work. The degree of freedom permitted a pupil should be gauged by his ability and willingness to accept the responsibilities accompanying it.

7/

The Social Development of the Educable Mentally Retarded Child

The educable retarded child's aptitude for social develop-ment. A large percentage of educable mentally retarded chil-dren may be trained to achieve a degree of social adaptability that exceeds their academic attainments. They can be taught to think not of themselves alone, but of others as well. They can be taught many rules of conduct that are generally regarded as evidence of good social behavior. Each child should be helped to develop a set of moral standards commensurate with his degree of understanding, and a set of desirable social habits. Habit will often serve the mentally retarded individual when understanding fails.

The responsibility of the school for social development. It is a major responsibility of the school to help the retardate become an acceptable member of home and society. Unless home influences are unstable or corruptive, the more fully the child participates as a member of his family group, the more likelihood there is that he will find some measure of security as a member of society.

The special class and the home. The teacher of a class of retarded children should endeavor to evaluate home influences exerted upon the children of his class, and teaching should be activated to strengthen the better influences and offset the less desirable ones. The teacher should try to solidify worthwhile habits and attitudes originating in the home, and endeavor to substitute desirable habits and attitudes for undesirable ones which may deter the retardate's social development.

The special class is a melting pot. The special class may be made up of children from widely different social, economic and intellectual backgrounds. Thus the special class represents a miniature society in which members with widely varying backgrounds and personalities are learning to live together. As they acquire attitudes of tolerance toward each other, develop habits of good conduct, and learn to live cooperatively together, they are fitting themselves for entrance into a larger society.

The importance of acceptance. Before the retardate can be expected to act in a socially acceptable manner, he must experience the feeling of being accepted by others. No matter what measure of rejection he encounters from his family, his neighbors, or pupils outside his own classroom, he must be made to feel that his classroom is a haven for him. Before the school can do much to mold his attitudes and habits into forms that will ease his acceptance by those outside his classroom, he must be made to feel that there he is a welcome and wanted member.

> Before entrance into a special class at the age of ten years, Mary had become known throughout the neighborhood as "The Brat." When she was between two and three years old, her mother had given birth to a boy. Mary showed a natural resentment and resistance when the younger child began to usurp her toys. She was reminded that her brother was "just a baby." When she refused to surrender her belongings to him she was punished. She responded by hiding and sometimes destroying his toys. On one occasion she cut up a cap which had been passed on to him when she outgrew it. As Mary grew older she began to take as her own any object belong-

ing to the neighborhood children to which she took a fancy. Rather than permit the object to be returned to its owner she would destroy it.

Shortly after Mary entered the special class her teacher noted her preference for a certain story book. The teacher made a point of reading to Mary from the book as frequently as she could. One day she suggested to Mary that she invite one or two of her classmates to sit with her and listen. Mary said, "No. Just me." Her teacher explained that she did not have time to read to as many children as she would like to. When Mary persisted in her attitude, her teacher said that the book would have to be put away until Mary was unselfish enough to share it with others. She placed it where it would be safe from Mary's destructive hands, and gave Mary a task to do which she hoped she would find interesting. The next day Mary chose two classmates to listen with her. Following the story hour, Mary's teacher thanked her, and, at the suggestion of the teacher, the two children also thanked her.

As Mary came to realize that her rights and privileges were respected by her classmates, her episodes of destructiveness became fewer and fewer. When, at the age of thirteen, Mary was placed in a private school, her teacher and her classmates were sincerely sorry to have her leave.

Gaining the confidence of the mentally retarded child. A mentally retarded child may come to the special classroom with a definite attitude of suspicion and distrust toward his teacher, his classmates, or both. He may show little inclination to cooperate with them, may resist the advances of others, or even show open antagonism. It may be that his experiences have been limited, and that he has known few people or places outside his home. Or, if he has been a school attendant, he may have had disagreeable experiences growing out of school failures, and perhaps have been subjected to ridicule and rejection by schoolmates. Whatever the reason for a child's unfriendly, uncooperative manner, he must learn to trust his teacher before much school progress, either socially or academically, may be expected. The teacher's warmth of personality, an attitude of faith in the child's ability to succeed, praise for every discernible bit of effort, and patient waiting may eventually be expected to produce good results in most cases.

The ability of the mental retardate to make social adjustments. There are many reasons why it is difficult for the individual of retarded mentality to make adequate social adjustments. Standards are set by persons of normal intelligence for persons of normal intelligence. The adult retardate is constantly thrown in with people of approximately the same chronological age and physical development, but with mental statures that exceed his own. Demands made are geared to the abilities of the majority. He lives within an environment which he often finds too complex for his full understanding. He does not learn from his experiences as readily as does the person of normal intelligence. He finds it difficult to consider all sides of a situation or to look below the surface for answers to his problems. He is relatively incapable of weighing the consequences of his actions. How well he anticipates the consequences of his actions will depend upon the complexity of the situation, as well as how often he has encountered similar situations. The hope that he will generally react in a socially approved manner is therefore dependent upon how permanent certain ways of conducting himself have become through habituation.

Becoming a social individual is a gradual process. Although, as suggested earlier in this chapter, an educable mental retardate may usually be trained beyond his mental age level, the social conduct of the younger and untrained child will usually be more closely allied to it. His transition from self-interest to group-interest is a gradual process. Like all children, he goes through a predominately "me" and "mine" stage, and he will remain longer at that stage than the average child of normal intelligence. The young retardate may demand all the blocks for himself rather than share them with another on a cooperative building project. He may want to get hold of the ball and keep it for himself rather than use it as an instrument of cooperative play. He needs to have toys that he can play with alone and activities that he can do by himself, as he is gradually taught that playing with others, although it may require the sharing of something, can often be more fun than playing alone. Gradually he may come to place group-interests before self-possessiveness.

Broadening social adjustments. Not only is the retarded child subjected to the demands of home and school, but also to the demands of his neighborhood play groups and, in time, to the demands of other community groups. In preparing pupils to meet group social demands, a teacher of a special class needs to ask certain questions. With whom does the retardate play in his out-of-school hours? Can he be taught certain games or stunts that will make him a welcome and useful playfellow? Does he have social contacts through his family or his church? Are there certain social amenities that can be taught him to ease his acceptance in those or other social groups? What can the school do to help him become socially integrated as he grows older? If his natural social milieu is a socially unhealthful one, what can be done to help him establish contacts that may advance his social growth?

Learning to be polite. Politeness may best be taught through exemplification, but added to this must be the opportunity to perform politely. The imitative qualities of the retardate will stand him in good stead if he has a well-liked teacher who is a model of politeness. As the child grows older and is called upon to meet social requirements foreign to the usual schoolroom situation, such as how to introduce one person to another, simulated situations may be used to teach him. The simulated experience should be used as a preliminary to practice in real life situations. Of course, the more often social habits are taught directly in the situations from which they originate, the better.

A class had been receiving instructions in the etiquette of introductions. One morning Dea's mother came to the classroom to discuss a matter with the teacher. The mother started to introduce herself when Dea jumped up and said, "I want to introduce my mother." The teacher asked Dea to come forward and make the introduction. This started a trend, and other pupils brought relatives and acquaintances to the schoolroom. Introductions were made to the class as a whole and, when it could be naturally arranged, to individual members. By the end of the school year the majority of the class were able to make introductions politely and without embarrassment.

Learning to be affable. Affability is a wonderful asset to a retardate. A cheerful, agreeable person who is eager to serve wins many friends. The feeling of friendship is a great stabilizer of conduct. As with politeness, the affability of a teacher is almost certain to be copied; an atmosphere of affability breeds affability in those exposed to it.

Learning to be honest. Honesty is an abstract term. The retardate needs to be taught to be honest in definite respects. The retardate cannot be expected to generalize the term. Some of the aspects of honesty that he needs to be specifically taught are:

Not to take things that belong to someone else.
To give back to their owners, or report or turn in, articles that have been found.
That cheating in schoolwork is dishonest.
That telling untruths is dishonest.
That one should do what is right even when he is not being watched.
To admit wrong doings.
Not to give false reasons because he thinks that it will better please his listeners or save him from punishment.

The school should provide an atmosphere that encourages the formation of good behavior patterns. If the school is to provide an atmosphere that encourages pupils to perform as cooperatively active members of the society which it represents, there are certain fundamental principles regarding pupil-teacher relationships that should be observed. Following are a few general suggestions for the maintenance of an emotionally healthful schoolroom atmosphere:

1. *Initiate a feeling of success.* Give the new entrant to a special class some relatively easy things to do, so that he may early acquire a feeling of success; see that each pupil has daily opportunity for a plentiful measure of it.
2. *Avoid the habit of failure.* This is a corollary of 1, above. Guide the pupil toward tasks within his ability of attainment. Frequently trying and then frequently failing destroys effort. Of course the child should be held to as high a level of attainment as his capabilities permit.
3. *Praise freely.* Be sure that each pupil receives a full measure of expressed approval. Praise for best effort as well as actual attainment.

4. *Expect the pupil to carry through tasks begun.* Assuming the pupil has been wisely guided in the choice of a problem or project so that it is neither too lengthy or too difficult, he should ordinarily be expected to carry it through to completion.

5. *Avoid making a child the obect of censure by his classmates.* Pointing out the faults of a child before a group may make him the object of ridicule by his classmates. As a result, resentments may be built up in the mind of the censured one and deter learning. Reprimands and corrective measures should be as privately administered as the situation permits. When the circumstance compels public correction, the manner of making the correction should be such as to discourage viewers from taking upon themselves to further punish the one under indictment. (These remarks are not to be construed as critical of self-governing student bodies if pupils are old enough and wise enough to suggest suitable disciplinary measures.)

6. *Make criticisms constructive.* Before giving it, be sure that adverse criticism is advisable. Having criticized, offer suggestions and see that opportunity is provided for improvement, and encourage autocriticism as far as it is constructively helpful.

7. *Teach obedience.* Only make rules that contribute to the smooth running of things. A few simply stated ones will ordinarily suffice. State requests positively and politely. Unless a choice is really implied, avoid asking "Would you like to . . . ?" Once a child has been told to do something, unless some unforeseen occurrence points out the injustice or imprudence of a request, he should be expected to do it. If there is a change, the pupil should be made aware of the reason for it.

8. *Avoid the habit of being unoccupied.* Probably more disciplinary problems grow out of failure to keep children actively engaged, mentally or manually, than in any other way. When a child has completed one task, there should be something else ready for him to do next.

Try to satisfy pupil requests. Insofar as a pupil's requests are reasonable they should be granted. When a request is denied and if the pupil is capable of understanding, a good reason should be given for the denial. Frequently some alternative may be suggested. Once a decision has been made, unless something arises that points out the injustice or unwisdom of it, it should remain unaltered.

Building a sense of worthwhileness. Optimum maturity cannot be reached by a retardate unless he feels that he is worthwhile. First, as has been suggested, he needs to feel confident within himself. He needs to be as self-reliant and act as independently as is prudently possible. If he is to attain independence of action, he must have tasks to do that are commensurate with his ability. He must have opportunities to do worthwhile things that contribute to the welfare of home and school and, as he grows older, of the community of which he is a part, and his contributions should be recognized and acknowledged in some manner. Until the feeling of worthwhileness has become well implanted, he needs frequent pats of approval to imbed it.

Ten year old Frank came to a special class after repeated failures in his school work. An examination had revealed his IQ to be 60. His parents were intelligent. His two siblings were star pupils in the school from which he was transferred. He had been censured for his failures by his parents. His brother and sister openly expressed their contempt for his low academic grades. They found no place for him in any of their out-of-school activities. He so utterly lacked confidence in himself, that when asked his name he would hang his head and reply almost inaudibly.

Upon entrance to his class Frank's new teacher welcomed him. Asking no response from him he introduced him to the class, indicating that the class was glad to have him as a member. At first it was only when his teacher took him by the hand and became a member of a play group with him that he would take any part in group activities. After a time the teacher began to substitute some classmate as Frank's play companion. In time Frank began to voluntarily take part in group activities. After a few months a new boy joined the class. When the teacher suggested that it would be nice if someone would show the newcomer around and see that he got acquainted, it was Frank who volunteered for the task.

SUGGESTED READINGS

SMITH, MARION F., with BURKS, ARTHUR J.: Teaching the Slow Learning Child. New York, Harper and Brothers, 1954.
Although in this book Mrs. Smith overly minimizes the need for a teacher of the mentally retarded to have as full knowledge as possible of the degree and nature of a child's retardation, she reveals herself as a dedicated teacher with more than average ability to deal with the emotional and personality problems of retarded children. She introduces the reader to specific experiences and specific individuals, and shows how she helped them to overcome feelings of inferiority, gain self-respect, and become socially efficient persons.

ILG, FRANCIS L., and AMES, LOUISE BATES: Child Behavior. New York, Harper and Brothers, 1955.
Although this book deals with the behavior of children in general, the principles it discusses are for the most part applicable also to the retarded child.

PETERSEN, SIGURD D.: Retarded Children: God's Children. Philadelphia, The Westminster Press, 1960.
This book is written by a psychiatric chaplain at a training center for mentally retarded children. The author does more than discuss the religious responses that may be expected from retarded children. He understandingly discusses their emotional make-ups. The book contains a number of case studies which illustrate the influences that environmental experiences have had upon the behavior of the individuals under discussion, and shows how understanding care and attention improved their thinking and actions.

8/

The Young Educable
Mental Retardate

Identifying the young retardate. This chapter is concerned with the chronologically young educable mental retardate who cannot perform as well as the average first grade entrant. He may be socially immature. He may not have learned to play well with other children of his own age group. He may not have learned to restrict his behavior sufficiently well to promote a high level of learning in the classroom. Because of either mental immaturity or environmental deprivations or both, he will not have acquired all the experiences necessary to have attained a state of readiness to learn to read.

A group of young retardates is made up of personality variants. No newly organized group of young mentally retarded children can be expected to start off as a completely harmonious and cooperative organization. Among entrants to a class may be those who have never before had an opportunity to play with other children. There will be those who have been overly protected and those to whom little direction or protection has been given. There will be children who are undisciplined and objectionably aggressive, and there will be those in whom feelings of rejection have been instilled. There will be those who know the security that comes from parental understanding, and those who do not. Any new entrant to a class of young retarded children must be treated as an individual before he can be expected to perform as a member of a group. Even the less asocial new entrant will find elements of strangeness in his new situation, and time may be needed for him to become adjusted.

Getting a group to work and play as a group. Until a child has gained a little self-confidence and a certain amount of self-direction, he cannot perform successfully as a member of a group. Forcing a child to enter into group activities while he is in a state of unreadiness is unwise. Overly persistent methods of trying to get a child to participate in group activities may only intensify his reluctance to do so, and cause him to draw farther into himself. It is better to let him get used to his surroundings, and allow some of the strangeness of his situation to wear off. He should have easy access to play materials which invite his use of them—steps to climb, blocks with which to build, crayons and paper for scribbling and drawing, or something else from the wealth of educational play materials available for use with children of nursery school or kindergarten age. As long as he is not disturbing others at work or play or performing acts of destruction, the young retardate should be allowed to move about and explore at will.

Helping the reticent young retardate to become more social. A kindly word of recognition now and then, a helping hand extended as needed, and an occasional invitation to do this or that may be effective. The child who hangs back from joining a group of skippers may feel more confident holding the hand of his teacher while skipping. After he has come to accept this partnership with confidence, the teacher may extend the free hand to another partner, and all three may skip together. Later the teacher may join the hands of the two children together, and drop out, leaving the two as partners. The child with backward social tendencies should be eased, not pushed, into group activities.

The size of play groups. Even within the relatively homogeneous group, as limited by IQ's and range of ages, there will be wide variations in play abilities. A child's degree of coordination, his previous play experiences, his personal likes and dislikes for other members of his group, and his ability and willingness to follow directions are some of the factors that influence his performances within a group. Sometimes a retardate who feels insecure in a large group may be able to perform well in a smaller one. He may perform well in a group of three or four, while he may seem totally at loss to know what to do in a group of ten or twelve. After he has learned to play well in a smaller group, he may be expected to adapt more readily to a larger one.

Objectives in the training of the young retardate. The objectives in the training of the young retardate should be:

To teach him to take care of himself, including his personal needs, as well as he can.

To help him to perform in as coordinated a manner as he can.

To help him to get about in, and become oriented within, as large an area as it is prudently safe for him to traverse.

To teach him such skills and knowledges as he is capable of learning that will be practically or recreationally useful to him.

To teach him how to use his leisure time.

To teach him to communicate with others as well as he can.

To teach him how to work and play with others.

To teach him how to become as socially efficient as his mental limitations will permit.

To build up a state of readiness for learning to read.

Sense training for the young retardate. The mentally retarded child needs to be taught to make the best use of his senses. Efficient use of the senses is more or less readily learned by children of normal intelligence, but the mentally retarded child needs definite instruction. The acuity of his senses cannot be increased through training, but the child can be helped to better discriminate. He can be helped to attain better habits of perception, and a more conscious and discriminative use of size, weight, color and form.

Training the sense of hearing. The untrained mentally retarded child is not usually a very attentive listener. Following are a few games intended to teach players to listen more attentively to achieve a better sense of sound direction, or to distinguish between differences in sound:

1. *A bell game.* Ring a bell in various parts of the room and at various heights, and have blindfolded children point to the part of the room from which the sound comes. When errors are made, have children remove blindfolds and look in the direction from which the sound comes at the same time they are listening.

2. *Bell the cat.* Blindfolded children try to catch an unblindfolded child who is running about ringing a bell. The one who catches the cat, then becomes the cat.

3. *Guess the voice.* One child is blindfolded. One at a time, children greet the blindfolded one, saying for example, "Good morning John." The blindfolded child tries to name the speaker. A score is kept of the number he guesses correctly. After his blindfold has been removed the unsuccessful guesser is allowed to look at the speaker as he or she greets him.

4. *Name the sound.* Blindfolded children may be asked to distinguish between the sounds of tapping with a light hammer on wood, on a glass tumbler, on the wall, on a hand bell, etc. Whistles, etc., also may be used. Children may be asked to distinguish between clapping, snapping fingers, stamping of a foot, etc.

5. *Magic music.* One player goes out of the room. The others then hide an object for him to find. When the child is called back, the teacher directs his movements by the piano. If the pupil is far away from the object she lets him know by playing very softly; as he gets nearer and nearer, the music becomes correspondingly louder.

6. *Music game.* A short strain of music is played over and over until the children become familiar with it. A part of a song they sing or a bit of music used with rhythms may be used. The strain is woven in with strains of music that are in marked contrast with it, and the children stand up, clap their hands, or in some manner indicate their recognition every time the familiar strain is played. If it is observed that some pupils are correctly responding because they are taking their clues from other pupils and not because they are attending to musical sounds, turns may be taken so that each child's listening powers can be tested.

Teaching color. A child may be able to distinguish between colors as proved by his ability to match colors, before he can identify them by their names. In the beginning it is better to place emphasis on one color at a time, adding colors as the child indicates he is able to differentiate between them and match like color with like. It is a good idea to start with some article for which a child has shown preference, as his favorite red toy or his new blue coat. He can be asked to find other articles of like color, which should be placed at different spots but within sight. The teacher may verbally associate the name of its color with each object as he finds it, and the child may echo the teacher's words, with possibly some resultant learning. It is just as well, however, to wait until he can optically distinguish between black and white and distinguish between the primary colors, before placing too much emphasis on the learning of their names. Below are a few games and devices which may suggest how to pleasurably teach color:

1. *Find objects.* Find and point to objects of a certain color in the room. Before the child has learned the names of colors, furnish an object to be matched in color. Later, naming the color will suffice.

2. *Picking out objects.* From an assortment of different colors pick out all of a certain color or sort according to color.

3. *Matching color.* The teacher holds up a card of a certain color, and asks the child to select a ball of the same color from a basket of balls of assorted colors. If he chooses the right ball he keeps it until the end of the game. At the end of the game the one with the most balls wins.

4. *Paper hats.* Children love to wear paper hats. They may be worn while marching or as a reward for a task well done. One day all may wear red hats, the next day all green, etc. Another day each child may choose his own color by naming it, or lots may be drawn from slips held in the teacher's hand. The colored portions of the partially colored slips are concealed. The child finds the colored hat he is to wear by matching the color he has drawn. On special occasions balloons may be matched to the hats worn.

Observing things. The retarded child may look at many things yet see but few. Following are a few games which may be of help to the teacher who is trying to teach young retardates to become more observant:

1. *What's in the room?* The children walk around the room, then take turns in telling things they have seen.

2. *What's in the picture?* At first the child looks and answers as the teacher points to objects in the picture and asks, "What's that?" Later, without the help of the teacher's pointing, the child names the things he sees in the picture. Finally he progresses to the point where, after looking at the picture for a time, he tells all the things he can remember having seen.

3. *Find the right pictures.* Each child is given four or five pictures of single objects. The teacher says, "Give me the dog," "Give me the girl," etc.

4. *A touch and name game.* Pupils are lined up for their turns, with those with the best memories in the front; those with poorer memories are placed in the rear so that they will have a longer time to memorize, and thereby lessen the likelihood of failure. The teacher names two plainly visible objects in the room. The first player in line runs, touches and names each object. If he remembers both he takes his seat in the front row which is for those who require only one trial. If he fails he goes back of the line of players so that he may have a second trial. Those requiring two turns sit in the second row, and so forth. As children become more adept the number of objects is increased.

5. *A touch game.* A player starts the game by touching an object. The next player touches that same object and also another. Each player touches those previously touched and adds another. When a player fails he is out of the game. The one who is able to correctly touch the most objects wins. Unfair competition may be controlled by giving those with weaker memories the earlier chances to play.

6. *Which order?* A limited number of objects are arranged in a row on a table. Pupils look at them for a time, noting the order of the arrangement. One pupil leaves the room. An object is taken out of the row and placed in a different position, and the objects shifted to make the spacing as before. The pupil is recalled and tries to put the row back in its original order.

7. *What's new?* A few objects are placed in view of the players. After looking at them carefully, they turn their backs while the teacher adds another object or two. The object of the game is to identify the added objects.

8. *Who's gone?* Three or four children stand in front of the playing group. The players close their eyes and turn around. One of the children in the line leaves the room. Pupils turn around and try to guess who is gone.

Training the sense of touch. Through tactile contacts the young retardate may be taught that things feel differently, and perhaps learn to make his sense of touch more useful to him.

Following are a few suggested ways of accomplishing this purpose:

1. *Recognizing solids.* First let the child look at a group of solids such as a cube, a sphere, a cone, etc. Have him turn around and put his hands behind him. Place one of the objects in his hands. After he has had a good chance to feel it, place the object back with the group, and have the child turn around and point to the one he has felt.

2. *Recognizing forms.* Played as in 1, above, except that squares, circles, triangles, etc., made of nonflexible materials, are substituted for the solids.

3. *Mystery bag.* The object of the game is to identify familiar objects placed in a cloth bag by feeling them. The inexperienced player will probably need to have objects exposed to his view before they are placed in the bag. The more distinct the shapes, the easier will be their identification.

4. *Who is it?* A blindfolded child may be asked to pick out a certain playfellow from the group by feeling for signs of identification—height, a necktie, a hair ribbon, beads or other item.

The young retardate and his speech. Not only will the young retardate come to school with a limited vocabulary, but in many cases the speech he does use will not be readily understandable. It is to be expected that a young retarded child will retain some of the infantilisms of speech longer than the average child of normal intelligence. The need for speech therapy is discussed in Chapter 10, "Teaching Language to the Mentally Retarded Child" (see page 82). Many retarded children need speech therapy if they are not to be deprived of communication with those about them.

Developing vocabularies. The young retardate never has enough words to express himself as satisfactorily as might be desired. He needs to see many things, handle many things, do many things, and then talk about the things he has seen and done. Pictures may be used to amplify vocabularies. It may be that to identify familiar objects by name is all that can be expected, but in time the child may reach a point where he can also tell what actions are taking place. It may take some time to get from the "Point to the boy," to the "What is that?"

stage. In muscular training the child walks "up the steps" and "down the steps"; he walks "along the line" on the floor; in games he rolls the ball "through the arch"; in target practice he aims "higher" and "lower." The young retardate needs to have language constantly tied to his activities.

Planned vocabulary additions. There should be constant checking on the part of the teacher to be sure the child is learning new words. Aside from words learned incidentally, concentration should be placed on one or two new commonplace words at a time, and daily practice should be provided until the child's own usage of them confirms that they have become a part of his vocabulary. He should have experiences to talk about, help in finding the right words to express himself, and ample opportunity for talking.

Handicraft work. Handicraft work for the young retardate has varied purposes—to improve finger dexterity and ability to handle things, to develop hand-eye coordination, and to furnish the child with types of occupations that may deliver him from the state of do-nothingness. The use of peg boards and bead stringing are time-honored occupations, but they should not be employed beyond the limits of their usefulness. At first, just putting beads on a string or fitting pegs in a board represents a successful degree of accomplishment. The use of color and design follows. Patterns may be traced and pictures colored, and of course the young child should have his chance to scribble and draw as his fancy suits. Eventually the young retardate may be called upon to draw pictures to illustrate a story heard or to illustrate something the child himself has seen or done. Finger painting is enjoyed by some. Inset puzzles and, later, the jigsaw type of picture puzzle will furnish occupation for some children. Puzzle pictures should portray things of interest to the child, should contain only a limited number of pieces, and should be simple in design. If the child can do some simple cutting, he should be provided with blunt-pointed scissors. It is suggested that he first be provided with forms outlined with broad lines that are easy to follow. If necessary, the teacher may more broadly outline pictures the child has chosen to cut out. Most construction and handwork activities suitable for children of nursery school or kindergarten age will be found suitable for use with young mentally retarded children. The more adept of the group may enjoy the use of simple looms.

Making scrap books. The making of scrap books has endless possibilities for young retardates. The child's first scrap book may serve merely as an exercise in cutting and pasting, without attention to whether or not pictures used are in any manner related. From the pictures he has cut out, the child may be helped to select one or two, which have been more carefully cut, to paste in his scrap book. The scrap book may be no more than two or three sheets of manila paper folded and somehow fastened together. After he has learned to cut without too badly mutilating a picture and to paste without too much messiness, his scrap books may become a little more organized in character. He may make an animal book, a dog book, a book showing children at play, one showing men at work, etc. In time he may be able to make a book in which a short picture story is told, as one that shows where Bobby went and what he did today.

Rhythmic play. Every class for retarded children should have a piano and someone to play it or a phonograph and some carefully chosen records. Rhythmic response to music is one of the best ways to help retarded youngsters learn how to use their muscles in a coordinated manner. Clapping to music, marching, and skipping are some of the simpler forms of responses. Marching calls for good standing postures. The "good soldier" stands "tall and straight." The monotony (although it may be the teacher rather than the pupil who feels it) may be broken by doing different things with the hands while marching, as clapping them rhythmically together, holding them high over the head or putting them on the hips. Bouncing a ball to music is a relatively difficult exercise. Even though not always perfectly performed by all, simple singing games which involve action are usually well liked. Stress should not be placed on learning the lyrics. It is usually better for the teacher to take the lead in the singing, with children chiming in when and if they can. In fact many of the words may have little meaning for the young child, even though he may enjoy repeating them in rote and rhythmic fashion.

Imitative rhythms. In addition to clapping, marching, skipping, and the like, there are any number of imitative activities which young children enjoy doing to music:

> Playing an imaginary piano is a good exercise to make fingers more nimble.
>
> Pounding nails like a carpenter.
>
> Rowing a boat or paddling a canoe.
>
> Pushing a swing.
>
> Driving an automobile.
>
> Playing train.
>
> Flying like birds.
>
> Prancing like horses in a parade.
>
> Hopping like frogs or toads.
>
> Playing elephant with arm swinging back and forth to represent the animal's trunk.
>
> Picking flowers or fruit, and placing them in a basket represented by a curved arm.

Need for muscular training. A child of normal intelligence usually acquires considerable dexterity in handling and manipulating things, and acquires needed balance and muscular control without specific training. A child of like chronological age, but who is below normal in intelligence, will usually have less control over the use of his muscles. He needs direction and practice to overcome his awkwardness and become able to handle and manipulate things with useful dexterity. The reader is referred to the list of muscular activities and stunts in the following chapter (see page 67).

Habits of usefulness. The young retardate should be taught habits of usefulness both to himself and others. The school should be equipped to help with his habits of personal cleanliness and neatness. There should be a lavatory close to the classroom. The child should have his own place to hang his wraps, and should know exactly where he is supposed to put his overshoes, mittens or other personal articles. There should be an area which is communally used and for which the child has the responsibility of keeping neat and orderly—a bookshelf, a reading table, a shelf where drawing supplies are kept, or he should have a schoolroom housekeeping chore which is definitely his own. He may be able to run small errands, pass supplies, or bring the broom and dust pan when needed. What the task is is not important, as long as the child recognizes it as something useful and accepts the responsibility for seeing that it is done when it should be done.

A list of desirable habits for the young retardate. The retardate, especially if he is of low mental age, is dependent upon habit for directing his behavior responses. It is well to have in mind some specific aims in habit formation for the young retardate. No child of normal intelligence performs perfectly, and certainly perfection is not to be expected of the retardate, but it is hoped a list may indicate the direction that habit training for the young retardate should take. Below are some specific habits worth striving for:

1. Come to school clean.
2. Come to school on time.
3. Wash hands after going to the toilet or when soiled.
4. Carry and use a handkerchief or paper tissue.
5. Keep fingernails clean.
6. Keep fingers out of mouth, eyes, ears and nose.
7. Brush teeth regularly.
8. Have regular toilet habits.
9. Know how to properly use drinking fountain.
10. Stand correctly.
11. Sit correctly.
12. Be tidy about eating.
13. Put suitable sized portions of food in mouth.
14. Keep mouth closed while chewing food.
15. Chew food well before swallowing.
16. Refrain from grabbing for food.
17. Ask for food politely and thank those who pass it.
18. Put articles of clothing away properly.

19. Put materials away after using.
20. Keep desks, tables, and adjoining floor space neat and tidy.
21. Play sociably with other children.
22. Greet, pass people, and enter a room politely.
23. Answer politely when addressed.
24. Refrain from taking the possessions of other children.
25. Refrain from pushing or striking other children.
26. Refrain from mutilating or destroying things.
27. Shut doors, move chairs, etc., with reasonable quietness.
28. Report damage to toys, materials and equipment.
29. Return found articles.
30. Know and respond to school signals.
31. Wait one's turn.
32. Be unselfish.

The young retardate in a group of more mature retardates.
Sometimes in a class of educable retardates there will be a single pupil whose interests and achievement are so immature that it is difficult to provide essential group training. The child seems to stand apart from the rest of the class. When a group project is under way the simplest of assignments (such as bringing a needed tool, helping to hold a board in place while another pupil is doing a bit of carpenter work, carrying something from one place to another, holding the dustpan in place during the sweeping up process, any simple task which goes along with the project under way) may serve to make him feel that he is a part of a working team. He may be taught some simple game or stunt, and at a recreational period the group as a whole may take a little time out from their own play projects to join in his play activity.

Added sources of help for the young retardate. Older pupils often quickly catch on to the fact that a younger pupil needs help, and willingly give their assistance in trying to fit him in as best they can with some of their less exacting activities. Sometimes an older pupil may be permitted to act as a teacher to his younger classmate; improper use of this practice, however, might encourage an aggressive older pupil to become overly domineering, but if properly supervised and cautiously used, it may prove to be socially beneficial to both. With the willing consent of the school principal and the kindergarten teacher a young retardate may sometimes be sent to the kindergarten classroom for a daily game or play period, giving him opportunity to learn more about how to play with others. The young retardate needs to learn how to work and play with others. He needs exercise both in individual and cooperative activities.

SUGGESTED READING

The following two books should be very helpful to the teacher who has young mental retardates in her class, but who is unfamiliar with the methods employed in nursery schools and kindergartens:

GANS, ROMA, ET AL.: Teaching Young Children in Nursery School, Kindergarten, and the Primary Grades. Yonkers, World Book Co., 1952.

WELLS, CLARA D., and STEGMAN, WILLIAM H.: Living in the Kindergarten: A Handbook for Kindergarten Teachers. Chicago, Follet Publishing Co., 1950.

PERRY, NATALIE: Teaching the Mentally Retarded Child. New York, Columbia University Press, 1960.
An invaluable book for the teacher of young mentally retarded children. It is written with the needs of the trainable retarded child in mind. Much of its material will apply to the needs of the educable mentally retarded child who has not yet reached the mental age, or acquired sufficient mental maturity, to be able to begin to learn to read. It is specific and filled with concrete suggestions. The appendix of the book lists educational materials, songs and games, children's books, and tells where they may be obtained.

GARTON, MELINDA DEAN: Teaching the Educable Mentally Retarded. Chapter 9: Audio-Visual and Other Sensory Training. Springfield, Ill., Charles C Thomas, 1961.
This chapter contains some practical suggestions concerning sensory training.

9/

Health and Physical Training for the Mentally Retarded Child

HEALTH TRAINING

Need for health training. Health is a major consideration for every child. The mentally retarded child is less capable than the child of normal intelligence of struggling against physical handicaps or ill health. By no means do all mentally retarded individuals come from homes where poor hygienic conditions exist, but many special class pupils do come from homes where health standards are less than desirable and where physical defects may go undetected and uncorrected.

The teacher's responsibility for guarding health needs. In the interests of the health of pupils the teacher of the mentally retarded has the following responsibilities:

1. To discover signs of physical irregularities.
2. To utilize means available to have symptoms properly diagnosed.
3. To make whatever classroom adjustments can be made to compensate for physical handicaps.
4. To control the schoolroom environment to the health advantage of pupils.

5. To furnish pupils with opportunities to acquire and practice health habits.

6. To encourage pupils to practice health habits outside the school.

7. To teach pupils to use community health services.

8. To try to instill a sense of pride in being a healthful person living in healthful surroundings.

Daily health inspection. Daily health inspections give the teacher an opportunity to detect signs of ill health that might require immediate attention, or conditions that should be checked to find if they are infectious or contagious. It is the time for checking on personal cleanliness and for observing evidences of regard or disregard for habits of health and cleanliness, over which the child has control. It is a time for commendation or for instruction if needed. Tactfully conducted, without embarrassing the pupil when calling attention to conditions for which he cannot rightfully be held responsible, health inspection may be made a period of learning.

Detection of chronic health conditions. The teacher should be alert for evidence of chronic conditions. The always tired and listless child, who seems to be growing too slowly, suggests a possibility of malnutrition or the need for a tuberculin test or chest X-ray. The child who gets out of breath easily and whose lips sometimes get blue may have a cardiac condition. Nervous conditions, hand tremors, twitchings of the head, face, or arm muscles, and dizzy spells are all symptoms indicating need for a medical checkup. The teacher should not assume the role of diagnostician, but he is in a strategic position to note important symptoms.

Visual defects. The teacher should be on the lookout for signs of sensory defects. In the child of normal intelligence, retardation in reading is often a sign of defective vision. In the case of the mentally retarded child it is taken for granted that he will be a backward reader, and even though he is reading and performing other tasks requiring vision less well than his intellectual potentialities could permit, poor vision often goes unnoticed as a contributing factor to his slow academic progress. Visual defects may be suspected if the child reads with his nose practically in the book, holds the book too far away when he reads, twists or turns his head to focus his vision, covers one eye when he reads, or often loses his place or tends to guess at words. The child with less than normal visual acuity often confuses letters in reading and spelling—o's as a's, e's as c's, n's as m's, n's as h's, m's as r's, or f's as t's.

Emergency symptoms. Constant rubbing of the eyes, constant protection of the eyes from the light by putting hands or arms before them, or prolonged or frequent headaches should be regarded as emergencies, as should any inflamed or sore conditions of the eyes until accounted for as not being of serious nature.

Testing visual acuity. Giving a preliminary test of visual acuity is a relatively simple procedure. Some states make it a legal obligation to have every school child's vision tested every year. If there are no school or community services provided for testing the visual acuity of pupils, the teacher should become acquainted with techniques involved. There will usually be some school or health agency willing to provide the needed simple apparatus and directions. If the tests reveal defects in visual acuity the child should be referred to someone who is qualified to make a diagnosis and to provide correction if necessary.

Hearing defects. There are symptoms which the teacher should note and interpret as possible indications of hearing losses. A hearing loss may be suspected if the child often wears a bewildered facial expression when he is in situations calling for hearing; if he frequently inquires, "Huh?" or "What?"; if he makes peculiar errors in spelling or written work; or if he speaks slovenly, omitting or substituting sounds. Children with running ears or who frequently complain about headaches should be referred for medical attention.

Schoolroom test of acuity of hearing. In some school systems pupils are regularly given audiometer tests to determine their hearing acuities. Lacking this service the special class teacher can make use of the watch test to screen out pupils who may be suspected of having hearing losses.

The face of a loud-ticking watch is placed to the examinee's right ear. He is asked if he can hear the ticking. Holding the watch at the same level from the floor, the examiner steps back a little at a time, stopping to ask the examinee if he can hear the ticking. The number of inches away from the examinee at which he first fails to hear the ticking is noted. This is done twice. Then the examiner starts at a point too far distant from the examinee for the ticking to be heard, and moves toward him. The number of inches from the examinee at which he is first able to hear the ticking is noted. This is done twice. The four findings are then averaged. For example if the distances are 16, 19, 18 and 19, the average will be 18. The normal distance from which a loud-ticking Ingersol watch may be heard is about 48 inches. The acuity of hearing for the examinee's right ear is recorded as R 18/48, which is not to be considered as a fraction but merely indicates that a sound that should normally be heard at 48 inches, has to be about 18 inches away from him before the examinee can hear it with his right ear. The same procedure should be followed for the left ear.

In their anxiety to please, or because they are not quite certain in their own minds, children will some times say they hear the ticking when they really do not; this may be checked by muffling the sound of the watch a number of times to determine if the child is reporting falsely. After a little kindly explanation, retesting may sometimes be necessary.

Procedures for obtaining diagnosis and remedial treatment. There will usually be established rules of procedures for dealing with children requiring immediate attention, as sending the child to the school nurse, reporting to the school principal, or the like. If the responsibility for seeing that something is immediately done is left entirely in the hands of the teacher the child may be sent home with a note, the parent may be telephoned to come and get a child, or whatever action the situation demands may be taken. The discovery of persistent symptoms indicating that some chronic condition exists should be reported and channeled through health agents provided by, or working cooperatively with, the school if such there be. Lacking this, consultation with a parent or parents is ordinarily the first step to be taken. If the family is unable to arrange for medical services needed or is indifferent toward the problem involved, parental consent can frequently be obtained to refer a child to the proper community health agency. The teacher should avoid representing himself as an authority capable of diagnosing the child's health needs, but the signs which indicate the need for medical attention can be pointed out. The teacher, however, is not overstepping bounds when warning against the use of eye glasses purchased at a ten-cent store, the employment of harmful home remedies, or the dependence upon the advice of known quacks.

Schoolroom adjustments to compensate for physical handicaps. Every effort should be made to compensate for whatever physical handicaps a child may possess. If it is indicated that rest periods should be provided, a cot may be set up in a well-ventilated cloakroom or supply closet. If the child has a heart condition the recommendations of his physician regarding types and amounts of exercise should be religiously followed, and the cooperation of the child's schoolmates should be solicited.

Adjustments to compensate for poor vision. Even though a pupil has had proper eye refraction, certain classroom adjustments may be beneficial to him. He should be permitted to move his desk so that he can see work on the chalkboard plainly. He should always be seated so that what he is reading or working upon is advantageously lighted. For reading, light should come from above and from the left, or from the right for left-handed pupils. The desk top should be adjusted to heights and angles that eliminate the necessity for bending over to see the printed symbols on a page. Rods may be used to keep books from slipping on a tilted desk. Proper seating, including proper adjustments, is essential to sight conservation. Poor vision causes poor posture, but poor posture can also cause poor vision.

The child should be protected from glare from polished surfaces on furniture and from glossy paper, either the pages of books or writing paper. For the child with extremely poor or failing vision, visually exacting manual tasks, as sewing fine seams, should be avoided.

Special print for the severely visually handicapped. If, even after refraction, a child appears to have difficulty seeing ordinary print, it is advisable to consult the child's eye doctor to find out if he should be reading large print as used in conservation of vision classes.

Adjustments to compensate for poor hearing. Classroom conditions should be made as favorable as possible for the child who is hard of hearing. If a hearing aid has been prescribed for a child, every reasonable effort should be made to see that he is outfitted with one. The teacher should learn how the instrument should be manipulated to be of most use to its wearer. The teacher should watch the child to see that he is wearing it and using it properly, and if necessary, teach him how to adjust and use the hearing aid to his best advantage. Some children are so-called "natural" lip readers, and learn the art with comparative ease, but this may not be expected of the mentally retarded child who will learn only through persistent and concentrated effort. Generally speaking, during a conversation with a hard of hearing child, it is better to reword a sentence than to resort to written language; but in the case of the retardate, if conversational and language building purposes are to be served, writing will need to be more generally used than would be the case with children of normal intelligence.

Conditions for easier lip reading. When addressing a hard of hearing person the speaker should enunciate, but should not use exaggerated, unnatural mouth movements. Unnaturally rigid or smiling lips are difficult to read. There should be no interfering shadows, and the speaker should be in a position where his face is in a good light and where the reader will have a full front view of it. The head should be kept reasonably still. Nods of approval and smiles should be inserted between spoken thoughts rather than included as a part of speech. If the school provides speech correction and hearing specialists, assistance may be had for the mentally retarded hard of hearing child.

The school should be a healthful place. Aside from the adaptations suggested to meet the special needs of the retardate handicapped by physical or sensory defects, the teacher has the responsibility of keeping the schoolroom environment a healthful place for the class as a whole. Equipment should be adjusted to prevent physical discomforts and defects. It is true that, with modern heating and ventilation systems, the teacher sometimes has little or no control over temperatures and air circulation, but, if he does, he should know what to do to control them to maintain a healthful classroom atmosphere.

Controlling lighting conditions and seating arrangements. The teacher should know what constitutes a properly lighted room. Whether the lighting conditions in the room are modern or less than modern, the teacher should know how to control existing lighting facilities to meet the varying needs that accompany the time of day or change of season, and to know how to provide the best lighting for the task at hand. It is not unusual to see shades improperly drawn, seating improperly arranged, and glare un-eliminated. Negligence has often been noted when it comes to finding the right seat for a child, and adjusting desks to fit the postural and visual needs of their occupants. Teachers should learn to use schoolroom equipment as the health and physical needs of pupils prescribe.

Health habits are acquired through specific instruction and opportunities for practice. Pupils should first be taught the degree of temperature that should be maintained in a classroom. They may then be permitted to check the room temperature on the classroom thermometer. They need to be taught how to adjust equipment to maintain the best possible lighting conditions in the classroom. Pupils may be given turns for the responsibility of adjusting shades to accommodate the needs of the class as a whole. Pupils, old enough to do so, should be made individually responsible for adjusting their own desks, and properly holding books so that light falls where it should— on books or work, and not in faces or eyes. Pupils should be taught to assume as much responsibility as they can for their own health protection.

The acquisition of habits of cleanliness. Habits of cleanliness are acquired only through the practice of keeping one's self, the things one uses, and one's environment clean. The teaching value of morning inspections depends upon the manner in which they are conducted. They should encourage the pupil to do better or to continue acceptably good practices. Learning is deterred when inspection causes undue embarrassment or resentment. It takes more than inspections to instill habits of cleanliness. Practice in keeping clean is also needed. When hands have become soiled in the process of an activity or when scrupulously clean hands are needed for a project to be undertaken, there should be a place provided, preferably within the classroom or an adjacent annex, where hands may be washed, where pupils may tidy up before lunch time, etc.

Specification has greater teaching value than symbolism. Correct dietary habits are more readily learned if specifically taught, than if taught in a vague, symbolic way. A personified Mr. Carrot or Mrs. Spinach will usually have little influence upon the eating habits of a young retardate. He needs to be taught to drink milk every day, include greens and vegetables in his diet, avoid eating too many sweets, and so forth. If school lunches are served they should exemplify dietary facts taught. Parental assistance, to the extent that parental intelligence and interest permit, should be utilized.

Teaching safety. Protection against accident may be considered as a health measure. As in the case of the instillation of other health habits, safety should be specifically rather than symbolically taught. However, simulated life situations may be used to dramatize certain safety precautions, as the use of STOP and GO signs, to supplement actual life situations. While the use of don'ts is often considered psychologically unwise, safety teaching sometimes demands it, for example, "Don't play with matches."

Acquainting retardates with community health services. Retardates should be helped to know what public health services are available to them and their families. If a mobile tuberculosis unit is coming to town or neighborhood, parental consent may be obtained to take the class or part of the class for the tests offered. Pupils may be taught the locations of public health agencies. In one known case, the teacher arranged for a visit to a health center, a health worker gave a short talk, and the children were given health literature to take home with them, as well as a set to be added to the classroom library.

Pride in good health should be a teaching goal. Mentally retarded pupils should be taught to have pride in their personal appearances, and to regard good health as an asset of which to be proud. When the class is going on a trip, the teacher may express pride in their appearances. The principal may ask for a strong healthy boy to help with a task requiring strength. The teacher may make some remark which connects his dietary habits with his fitness for the job. Recognition should be given for efforts to maintain standards of healthfulness.

PHYSICAL TRAINING

The need for physical training for the mentally retarded. Although retardates as a group are below average in muscular control and coordination, there are many of them, particularly if they approach borderline intelligence, who cannot be singled out in their own chronological age group by their poor muscular responses. For those who need it, however, first attention should be given to overcoming, as far as possible, poor postures and awkward movements which tend to accentuate their backwardness.

Physical training with regular grade pupils. Whenever a special class pupil can take his place in a regular gymnasium class without being unduly conspicuous he should be allowed to do so provided, of course, that the supervisor's and the teacher's cooperation may be obtained. The pupil should then follow the regular practices of the group in which he is enrolled. His placement should depend upon his ability to understand directions and profit from the instruction given, and upon the degree of his acceptance by the members of the group in which he is enrolled.

Physical training in the special class. There will be pupils, who because of physical infirmities, exaggerated lack of muscular control, or inability to grasp directions, will need to take their gymnasium work with their regular classroom group, preferably in the school gymnasium at a period set aside for their use. If no assistance is provided in the way of definite supervision of activities, the teacher may need to rely upon the aid of manuals or instructional books. Activities should be chosen with the particular needs of pupils in mind. Verbal directions should be as simple and direct as possible, and as frequently repeated as necessary.

Self-play and follow-the-leader stunts. The following activities, taken from the author's book, "The Mentally Retarded Child and His Parent,"* are suggested for training in muscular coordination:

1. *Walking stunts:* Walking straight or circular lines; draw chalk lines on the floor.
   Stepping over objects.
   Walking around objects placed as obstacles without hitting them.
   Starting with right foot; starting with left.
   Going up and down stairs properly.
   Marching.
   Walking on rounds and sides of ladder placed flat on the ground.
   Series of boxes; stepping from box to floor and floor to box without looking at feet.

2. *Jumping:* Jumping lines.
   Jumping rope.
   Hopping from point to point on both feet without losing balance.

---

* Slaughter, Stella S.: The Mentally Retarded Child and His Parent. New York, Harper and Brothers, 1960, p. 60 ff.

Hopping on one foot from point to point.
Hopping on one foot and keeping on a chalked line.
Hopping with arms folded.
Hopping with arms back of head.
Hopping to avoid ball rolled and aimed at feet.

3. *Stunts with balancing board:* Walking across, using cane to assist.
Walking across using balancing pole.
Walking across with arms folded.
Walking across with object on head.
Walking across with fewest steps possible.
Wheeling a toy wheelbarrow across.
Carrying a tray with a tower of blocks on it.

4. *Slapping:* Try to hit the extended hands of another person with a piece of cardboard before the person can withdraw his hands.
Bean Porridge Hot. (In the beginning use only the motion accompanying the first three words of the verse.)

5. *Picking up:* Using buttons, blocks, seeds, pieces of paper, etc., see how many objects can be picked up in one minute, and so forth.

6. *Wringing:* Race with time or another person to see how many Mason jar tops can be removed.
Twirl button molds on a string.
Spin tops.
Spin pie plates.

7. *Throwing:* Bean bags in a box or basket.
Target games.
Ringing a stake. To begin with, it is suggested that ring be of as large a size as can be conveniently handled.
Playing catch.

8. *Pushing and pulling:* Push and pull toys: balancing ball, wheelbarrow, kiddie car, carts, toy trains and wagons, rocking horse, hoops, pushmobile.

9. *Stunts involving carrying objects in hands:* Carrying an object in one hand (anything from a book to a container filled with water) while the other hand is: holding another's hand, moving a chair, opening a door.

10. *Manipulation of hand muscles:* Bead stringing.
Putting pegs in boards.
Drawing and painting.
Cutting out pictures.
Using sand, clay, and plastic materials.
Tearing carpet rags.
Buttoning clothes.
Lacing shoes.
Braiding.
Using hand punch.

Play activities. Formal gymnastics should not be regarded as a substitute for indoor or outdoor recreational activities. Balancing boards, steps to climb, balls for indoor use, or other simple play apparatus, which allow practice in body balance and muscular control should be available and used. Folk games and indoor competitive games have value as group activities for periods of relaxation and for overcoming awkwardness of movement and clumsy manipulation. The retardate who has the ability to make the school baseball team, or enter into some type of competitive athletics, should not be denied the opportunity to compete for a place.

Playground supervision. The playground is an excellent place for learning activities which may be transferred to the retardate's out-of-school living, and provide him with healthful leisure time outlets. Supervision must be relied upon to extend the variety of recreational activities and to suggest substitute activities to replace undesirable ones. Supervision must also be relied upon to help the individual who does not voluntarily attach himself to some play group and find that group whose play interests most closely coincide with his own.

Direction is sometimes needed. Pupils should be encouraged to select and direct their own play activities, which should be given preference over those selected by the teacher as long as the activities contribute to the play maturity of the group as a whole. When self-direction is lacking, however, or activities become stagnantly repetitious, the playground supervisor should be prepared to suggest new games or activities. The playground is the natural melting pot for retardates and non-retardates, the place where the retardate is most apt to find acceptance by his fellow schoolmates.

Meeting the needs of the more mature pupils. It has already been suggested that when and where feasible, the retarded pupil should be permitted membership in physical education and recreation groups with children of normal intelligence. As the educable retardate becomes more physically and socially mature the average teacher of the mentally retarded becomes less qualified adequately to meet his physical education needs. The well-trained physical education instructor is concerned both with the physical and social development of pupils. He usually has contact with a large area of the school's population, and is therefore acquainted with the situations where the retarded pupil will best fit in. On the basis of information furnished by the pupil's teacher the physical education instructor can place the child with that group or groups best suited to his needs in terms of physical betterment, recreational opportunity and social development.

SUGGESTED READING

LA SALLE, DOROTHY: Guidance of Children Through Physical Education, 2nd ed. New York, Ronald Press Co., 1957.

This book does more than list and give directions for performing certain physical activities. It considers the differing physical needs of children, and emphasizes the use of physical education to promote both physical and social development.

10/

Teaching Language to the Mentally Retarded Child

Retardates are limited in their language abilities. "Given the best environments and the best teaching guide, the mentally retarded child will be backward in his language development."* There is a close relationship between intelligence and language usage. However, environmental language deficiencies and inadequacy of instruction limit the language learnings of a large percentage of mental retardates to a greater than necessary degree.

Home influence on language learnings. Most retarded entrants to a special class come with a lesser knowledge of language meanings than inherent capacities would permit. Not only is this true when children come from poor intellectual backgrounds, but also when retardates come from average or above average intellectual environments. Because of his child's slow linguistic progress, a parent may become discouraged and curtail his teaching efforts perhaps at the very point where, if instruction were continued, the child would begin to use words more abundantly. Sometimes a large proportion of the lan-

---

* Ingram, Christine: Education of the Slow-Learning Child. New York, World Book Co., 1960.

guage of his environment is beyond the child's comprehension. Unless an effort is made to convert some of the family talk into understandable language for him—particularly when the topics of conversation are of interest to the child—he may feel left out and find no real incentive for trying to talk. The school must start where the child is in his language development.

The importance of language. Language is an often neglected subject with retarded children. Perhaps because its importance is less patent than certain other school subjects, it is not uncommon for a teacher to neglect its teaching if more time seems to be required to complete other school tasks. If something must be omitted from the day's planned work, it is often language that is left untaught. The value of language, particularly oral language, may be hidden, but it is often of more importance than that for which it is omitted. The "three R's" are often spoken of as if they were the three all-important educational necessities, yet language is a prerequisite for each of these, and no amount of reading, writing, or arithmetic may be learned apart from language. What is even more important, a retardate's opportunities for social integration are greatly influenced by his ability to use oral language. If he cannot understand what others are saying, if he cannot enter into some of the conversations of any given social group, his chance to become an active member of that group is cancelled.

Language and thinking. As has been indicated elsewhere in the book the mental retardate is more concrete-minded than verbal-minded. Verbal thinking, however, is not to be entirely ruled out as an asset to him. He will never become a profound abstract thinker, but he should be helped to think verbally as maturely as he can. The more word meanings he has, the more verbal thinking he will be able to do.

Talking helps verbal thinking. Children of preschool age do quite a lot of verbal thinking; their talking and thinking go on simultaneously. The same is true of the young retardate if he has a chance to talk. Opportunities for talking encourage verbal thinking. The exception to this statement is the occasional mentally retarded child who talks a good deal but does not use language comprehensively. He is a parrotlike echoer of other people's speech. His habit may be based on a paucity of experiences to talk about or on a lack of opportunity to talk about them. Given a chance to experience and talk about things, he may in time overcome his debilitating habit. If the tendency (when persistent it is called *echolalia*) does not disappear after remedial teaching, the case should be referred for clinical study.

Language should be taught functionally. Language for the retarded child is best taught in situations where language is naturally used. Teaching by having the pupil recite set arrangements of words, as the rote recital of a story, reciting a speech composed by some one other than the speaker, or giving set answers to questions, discourages rather than encourages a pupil to become a conversationalist and use language to convey his own thoughts. Using language in natural life situations, talking about things that have interest and meaning for the speakers, will result in far greater spontaneity of speech. Too often emphasis in language training is placed on getting the pupil to talk as the teacher wants him to talk, and too seldom on getting him to express his thoughts. Too often stilted classroom language exercises implant in the pupil a fear of, or at least a dislike for, expressing himself.

Functional topics of discussion. Assuming their relationship to the lives of their discussers, the following topics for informal classroom discussions are illustratively suggested:

School activities—both schoolroom and playground.
Outside activities—pets, gardens, vacations, playmates and leisure time.
Occupations of the various members of the family, and of relatives, friends, neighbors, and other people in the community.
Class and individual excursions.
Giving directions for how to get somewhere.
Explaining how something is done or a game is played.
Health and safety discussions.
Names, qualities, and uses of materials, tools, and equipment used in shopwork, cooking, sewing, etc.

Speech standards. Standards of speech for the retardate should be based chiefly on standards acceptable to the social group of which he is and will be a part. Acceptable standards are not likely to be very rigid. Prepositions at the ends of sentences or the use of split infinitives would be quite sure to go unobserved. He may or may not be looked at with eyes askance if he talks about "them apples."

Correction of errors. Avoidance of errors is better than correction of errors, but even if the teacher's own enunciation, pronunciation, and grammatical usage are exemplary, she may not expect to wholly combat the effects of undesirable out-of-school influences. Gross errors should be corrected to the extent that the time spent in making the corrections is justified, and to the extent that corrections do not interfere with the desire to talk. It is better to allow a child to finish his sentence or story before pointing out his errors than to constantly distract his attention from what he is saying because of insistence on how he is saying it. If a single error can be quickly corrected without obtruding upon thought, the immediacy of the correction has teaching value. After his errors have been pointed out to him, he can repeat a part of his conversation or story correcting his previous mistakes. An expression of approval for having told his story even better than before may help to establish the correct speech habits. If the retardate is showing improvement in his speech habits, is continuing his interest in wanting to talk and is adding new words to his vocabulary and new topics to his conversation, it may be considered that he is doing very well indeed.

Talking should come before writing. The first step in the language development of the mentally retarded child should be experience, and the second step the opportunity to talk about experiences. Speech is a more plastic form of expression than writing and is a form more often needed. His written expression will be better and his language development further advanced if things to be written about at length are discussed and if ideas are expressed verbally before their written expression is attempted. Throughout his life there will be a more predominate need for talking than for writing, and the school should take this into consideration when planning language instruction for the retardate.

Written language. The needs for written language in the adult life of the retardate are few. Occasionally filling out forms, making lists of things to be remembered and writing letters about cover his necessities. In the areas of these needs he should have practice before leaving school. He should learn to write simple friendly letters without conversational rehearsals. He should have practice in filling out such forms as may be required of him as an adult.

Classroom uses for written language. Below are suggested classroom activities utilizing written language:

1. *Notices.* Pupils may compose briefly worded notices to put on the bulletin board—lost and found notices, for sale ads, classroom announcements, notices of outside events which may have special interest for readers of the bulletin board.

2. *Stories.* Pupils may write stories about a class excursion or other interesting experience. A single sentence will suffice for the beginner. The sentence may in itself be a story or it may be a contribution to a class composite story. It will be the exceptional retardate who will want to expand his composition beyond a couple of paragraphs at one writing.

3. *Classroom newspapers.* A classroom newspaper published at convenient intervals is an excellent device for stimulating interest in wanting to write. News items about things that have happened and things to come, notices, ads, any matters of class interest may be written into its pages. Each pupil may contribute according to his ability. The final publication may be handwritten, typewritten, or mimeographed.

4. *Notebooks and diaries.* Notebooks may be kept for recording facts about a classroom activity or used in connection with a social studies project. Personal or classroom diaries may be kept. Personal diaries kept over a period of time help to reveal to the pupil his own progress in language and writing.

5. *Letter writing.* Three types of letters for which a retardate may have need are: (a) Friendly letters to relatives, friends, classmates who are ill, members of classes in other cities, etc.; (b) invitations to parties, parents' meetings, assembly programs, etc.; (c) business letters to order things, to ask for information, to apply for employment, etc.

Before he leaves school the retardate should have practice in those forms of letter writing for which he will probably have use. He should be taught how to properly address letters. He should be furnished with samples of the types of business letters for which he will have probable use, and should have practice in the writing of such letters.

6. *Filling out forms.* Shortly before the potentially employable retardate plans to leave school to take his place in the outside world, he should receive instruction in the proper filling out of applications and other forms in common use. Questions should be taken from forms in current use in the community.

The use of punctuation by the mentally retarded pupil. Punctuation should be kept as simple as possible for the mentally retarded pupil. One-clause sentences should answer most of his written needs. Rather than trying to get him to use complex sentences in his writing, it is better to use the time to enrich his vocabulary. The use of one-clause sentences results in fewer errors in punctuation. It is not easy to teach the mentally retarded child the proper use of commas, semicolons and quotation marks. It is wiser to concentrate on the use of capitals at the beginning and periods or question marks at the end of sentences and possibly the use of commas between series of words. The teaching of other forms of punctuation should be delayed until these simple forms have been mastered. The written work of the teacher which comes to the eyes of the pupils should, of course, be free from error.

Building vocabularies. Added experiences mean opportunities for additions to vocabularies. If the experiences are talked about, new word meanings may be derived from them. Group discussions afford opportunities to indicate how the same idea may be differently expressed. If two pupils express the same idea in different language, attention may be called to this fact. The teacher might say, "You notice that Tom spoke about a 'good time,' and Mary about a 'nice time,' and we might call it a 'pleasant time,' too." If a pupil describes an elephant as "awful big," the teacher could agree by saying, "Yes, it is a huge animal." Words should be selected for inclusion in vocabularies and should be firmly implanted through repetitious use.

If the word being taught is "pleasant," reference one day may be made to the "pleasant weather," the next day to a "pleasant journey," and on Monday to a "pleasant weekend." Reading, unfortunately, adds comparatively few words to the speaking vocabularies of most retardates. If words are to become a part of a retardate's spoken vocabulary, he must hear them often, and verbally repeat them often enough so that they become fixed verbal habits.

Story telling for the mentally retarded child. Stories told to the mentally retarded child should be of interest to him and worded in language comprehensible to him. When the language of an otherwise suitable story is too difficult to be understood by him, it should be simplified to agree with his level of understanding. Stories should contain more familiar than unfamiliar elements. Imaginative stories should be used only when it is certain that listeners are capable of distinguishing between the make-believe and the real.

Getting the moral of the story. If a mentally retarded child is to understand the moral implications of a story, ideas should be presented concretely rather than abstractly. The things the characters in a story do and say should be worthy of emulation. Even though they are placed in a story to teach by way of contrast, it is better not to place emphasis on acts of cruelty, dishonesty, or other undesirable behavior. The retardate is apt to entirely miss the moral lesson, to remember only what the characters of the story did and said, and to copy that which catches his attention and intrigues his interest, be it good or bad.

Retelling of stories. Stories chosen for retelling by individual pupils should be brief. The retelling of longer stories is best handled as a group project. Even then it is wise not to choose a story that goes on and on. When stories are retold by a group, the teacher may step in as occasion demands to keep the story moving in the right direction and at a rate of speed that will bring the story to its conclusion within a reasonable length of time. The teacher's questions may invite the responses of non-volunteers. "Tell us what Peter did next," or "Something exciting happened then. What was it?" When responses have to be pressured from the group as a whole, it may be assumed that the story chosen is not a suitable one, at least not as a story to be retold.

The use of pantomime for the development of language. Pantomime may be used to encourage the use of language. One individual is selected to do the miming, and the remainder of the group try to guess what is being portrayed. At the start, the imitations should be simple commonplace activities or easily identified movements such as sewing, hanging up clothes, hoeing, raking leaves, driving an automobile or flying like a bird.

Older children may sometimes be encouraged to vary their language and use somewhat more complex phrases if a list of ideas for pantomiming is written on the chalkboard. A child or, if need be to get the game started, the teacher may act out one of the phrases listed. The others try to choose and repeat from the list on the chalkboard the correct phrase to fit the action. To illustrate, the list might read:

> a housewife washing and drying dishes
> a fisherman baiting his hook and catching a fish
> a cowboy on a bucking broncho
> a leader of a band
> a person boarding a bus
> a ticket seller at a theater

Although the manner of expression may be new to the player, the activity represented should not be new.

Dramatization for the mentally retarded pupil. There may be times when it is desirable for a retarded child to learn set lines so that he may take part in a school assembly or appear before an audience. The social values involved may be of considerable importance to the performer, but the amount of improvement in language may be expected to be negligible. When the dialogue is made up of lines remembered because they have captured the interest of a story listener or reader together with lines of his own composition, much more influence upon his speech habits may be expected. The dramatization of a favorite story, keeping to the dialogue only as interest and memory prompt and adding original dialogue as the action of the performance demands, will advance the language learnings of the retarded child much greater than where memory alone is the essential for successful performances. Questions may need to be asked by the teacher to stimulate thinking: "Do you remember what Roger asked the old man?" "What do you think he said when he got there?" etc. If the performance is to be perfected for public presentation, lines may need to be written down and learned.

Dramatization of commonplace happenings. Although complete transfer from simulated to real life situations may not be expected, dramatization may be effectively used to help the retardate know what to say, and how to say it, in some of the ordinary situations he will probably encounter. For the younger child, playing store, visiting, and talking on toy telephones are means of getting him to talk. Although a few conversational amenities may be casually introduced, correct speech forms should not be insisted upon at the expense of loquacity.

Training the retardate to meet specific situations involving the use of language. As the retardate grows older, he will encounter many situations which need to be verbally met. Often it is not easy for him to know how to meet these demands courteously and efficiently. If the dramatization of these commonplace situations can be followed by opportunity to use in real life situations what he has been practicing through dramatization, his learning of the correct habits will be better assured. It is important that a retardate be able to state his wants and needs with clarity and courtesy in his every day living.

Some common life situations requiring speech. Below are listed a few life situations which lend themselves to dramatization:

Use of the telephone—properly addressing persons called; properly responding when called; getting the desired information with expediency; calling the doctor, the police, or the fire department.

Having guests for a meal.

Ordering a meal in a restaurant.

Asking for a book at the library.

Buying a ticket for a journey.

Renting a house.

Applying for a job.

Language games. Many language games are not as educational as they are intended to be. Much time devoted to them may later prove to have been wasted when the pupil, confronted with natural situations, continues in the same old habits which the games were supposed to correct. The pupil may connect the approved form only to the game situation. The teacher should carefully analyze language games before adopting them for class use. All games which use stilted or stereotyped forms of responses should be avoided. To be useful a game should require that a child be obliged to think before he answers. A game which permits variation in responses, rather than one in which the response is a choice between two answers, is more apt to have teaching value.

A preposition game. Retardates usually do not use prepositions freely. The following game is intended to encourage their use.

The teacher places on the chalkboard a list of prepositions—*as, on, in, beside, under.* Some small article is hidden within a prescribed area. The guesser tries to locate it by questioning, "Is it *in* the vase?" "Is it *under* the book?" etc., each time using one of the prepositions listed.

Descriptive word game. The retardate's use of descriptive words is usually repetitive and unimaginative. The following game is intended to help him learn new descriptive words and add variation to his speech.

From a group of objects one, known to all but the guesser, is chosen. On the chalkboard is written a list of descriptive words or phrases, only one of which adequately describes the object selected. The guesser questions one pupil after another, incorporating in his questions one of the descriptive terms such as: "Is it *useful*." "Is it made of *metal*?" "Is it *fragile*?" He is not allowed to attempt to name the object until he gets an affirmative answer to a question.

Verbal treasure hunt. This is a somewhat more difficult game to play than the ones previously described. It requires more thinking on the part of the questioner, and opens up the opportunity for practice in word usage. It is a game that may narrow or widen in scope to fit the abilities of the players.

An object is hidden. The guesser begins by trying to narrow down the area in which it is hidden by asking questions such as: "Is it somewhere in this building?" "Is it in this room?" "Is it in somebody's desk?" "Is it on top of the desk?" Sometimes the teacher should have a turn at guessing, and use it as a chance to suggest a word or two that has not been used before: "Is it in the *northeast* corner of the room?" "Is it near the *ceiling*?"

Better-speech bulletin board. When one pupil detects an error in the speech of another he may prepare a notice which, as soon as it has passed the teacher's inspection, may be placed on the speech bulletin board. As an example: *Kenneth* (using the name of the pupil who made the error)—*I haven't any pencil.* Only correct forms should appear on the board. Such a device is good only to the extent that it is accepted without resentment by those criticized. If some pupil's name appears on the board, and yet he is never responsible for the detection of errors in his classmates, the teacher may confidentially call his attention to the error of another pupil, particularly one whose errors go unchallenged. If the challenger has difficulty in preparing his notices, the teacher may lend him assistance.

The study of grammar for the retardate. The only way a mentally retarded individual may be expected to learn to speak and write correctly is through the repetitious use of speech and writing in situations that have meaning for him. Speech is a matter of habit. He may be able to learn the names of the different parts of speech, but he will not become adept at identifying them in sentences. The time he spends doing it will have negligible, if any, influence upon his own speech habits. He may be able to repeat certain rules of syntax, yet be entirely unable to apply them. The study of grammar as a formal subject is a waste of time for the retardate.

Speech defects in the mentally retarded. Some years ago a three-year study was made in the Rochester, New York, schools. As a result of this study, it was estimated that 12 to 13 per cent of special class pupils in the Rochester schools had speech defects, including infantile speech, lisping, and stammering. In the regular grades the rate was only 2 to 3 per cent. Mentally retarded pupils with speech defects should be referred to a speech therapist if one is available. It is unwise for a teacher without special training in speech to employ exercises or speech corrective techniques unless she is acting under the advice of a trained specialist. Whatever advice is offered should be conscientiously followed. Faulty instructions to children with speech difficulties may only serve to set patterns or, possibly, to saddle a child with feelings of nervousness or nervous tics.

General suggestions for the classroom treatment of speech defects. The main needs of a retarded child with infantile speech may be the chance to live in an environment that fosters speech growth, and time enough to grow out of the habit. The teacher can set the example of good speech, and can add words of encouragement as opportunity is afforded. When a speech defective has spoken in a better than usual manner the teacher may say, without reference to his defect, "How well you said that." The teacher should always refrain from making embarrassing remarks that call attention to a child's difficulty. The main therapy is the creation of a mentally healthful atmosphere. If a child can be spared embarrassment, can have the opportunity to build up feelings of confidence in areas that do not overemphasize the use of speech, and can be helped to feel happy and secure, his chances for speech improvement will be multiplied. It is in this same manner that the chronic speech defective must be taught to learn to live as comfortably as he can with his difficulty.

SUGGESTED READING

STRICKLAND, RUTH G.: The Language Arts in the Elementary Schools. Boston, D. C. Heath and Co., 1957.

This book, touching on all phases of language development, including reading, writing, and spelling, is concerned with helping children "develop the ability to communicate effectively." While the book's material applies to the child of normal or gifted intelligence (there are a few specific references to the mentally retarded child), much of what is said about language for the child of primary school age is applicable to the mentally retarded child of like mental level.

11/

Teaching Reading
to the Mentally
Retarded Child

The reading needs of the mental retardate. The reading
needs of the mental retardate are threefold:

1. *The practical need:* There are practical reasons why every individual
   capable of acquiring any degree of reading ability should learn to
   read. He needs reading to live efficiently and safely. He needs
   reading to help him move about safely and independently in his
   community and wherever else his travels may take him. He needs
   reading to help him get the informational and directional knowledges
   necessary to carry on hobby, home, and occupational projects. He
   should be able to read the advertisements that tell him where the
   best place is to buy the things he needs or wants at the prices he
   can afford to pay, or where employment is available when he is in
   need of employment.

2. *The social need:* Reading has a social as well as practical value for
   the mentally retarded individual. It affords him a certain amount
   of prestige, and he derives social satisfaction from it. Observation
   has shown that the child who does not know how to read as well
   as his classmates is quickly dubbed a "dummy," and there is no
   other school subject that accentuates his lack of intelligence as
   pointedly as reading does. When a child can show mastery over
   reading symbols he gains importance in the eyes of himself and his
   fellows. His reading as an adult will not include the perusal of

editorials, but he may get enough from the headlines of the daily newspapers to allow him to put in his two cents worth when topics of the day are being discussed. He may be able to do no more than express approval or disapproval of some person in the news, or to pronounce that some happening is "awful," but if his experience has made him feel a part of a conversational group, it has served a social purpose for him.

3. *The recreational need:* It should be demonstrated to the retardate how reading may contribute to his leisure time pleasure by learning how to read directions for carrying out hobby interests, finding out how to play certain games, etc. He needs reading to find when his favorite TV or radio program may be expected. He needs to be guided in his selection of books and magazines, with the thought in mind of perpetuating his reading interests. Magazines that are largely pictorial in nature may capture his interest. Stories with simple plots and those involving action and adventure may appeal to some older retardates. A retardate may not spend many of his leisure hours reading just for fun, but he should be shown where to find suitable reading to satisfy whatever worthwhile reading interests he may have.

Progressive steps in the teaching of reading to the mentally retarded:

Step 1. In the beginning stage of reading there is more talking than reading. This is where the idea should be established in the mind of the would-be reader that reading, like talking, is a medium for the expression of thought. Sight words are used —names are attached to articles of ownership, labels are placed on containers of supplies and other objects in the room. Action words are developed through activities and observation, and connections established with printed symbols. Experience stories are written on the chalkboard. As the teacher reads back, and underscores with hand or pointer, the child repeats any word or phrase he recognizes at sight. However, there should be no drilling on word recognition at this stage. It is far more important that a pupil be able to comprehend meanings than be able to recognize words at sight. He needs to learn that printed symbols can tell a story. This idea is further strengthened when his teacher reads him stories that he enjoys.

Step 2. At this stage the child is beginning to build up a sight vocabulary—to be able to recognize some printed words without dependence upon pictures or other clues, or help from his teacher. He is beginning to use books, progressing from the pre-primer or primer to the first grade level of reading. He is reading more and more independently, without the aid of crutches or constant teacher supervision.

Step 3. This is the stage of reading where, after having acquired a concept of reading as a thought-getting process and having acquired a sizable vocabulary of sight words, the pupil will ordinarily be ready to apply phonetic analysis in deciphering new words. He may have had some practice in listening to and identifying speech sounds, but now he is increasing his knowledge of, and systematically attempting to use, phonetic techniques to increase his reading vocabulary without dependence upon sight alone.

Step 4. At this stage reading increasingly becomes a tool for learning new things. Not only is the pupil reading about things he has already observed or experienced or that have story value for him, but he is also using reading to gain new informations and to find out how to do things. His reading will have more than transitory value. Some of the things he reads he will want to remember. Practical information that will aid him in the mastery of his environment should be added; reading that is newsworthy should be encouraged. And now is the time for the pupil to get acquainted with the leisure-time possibilities of reading.

Methods of teaching reading to the mentally retarded. There is no so-called best method especially applicable to the reading needs of the mentally retarded. Methods of teaching reading applicable to children of normal intelligence are generally applicable to mentally retarded children capable of learning to read. The development of skill in reading is a complex process, subject to a wide range of individual differences and dependent upon a number of factors. What works with one pupil may not work as well with another. The experience approach is widely regarded as a good way to start the beginning reader, and well supplements most commonly used methods of teaching reading. At all stages of the mentally retarded reader's development a goodly proportion of his reading should be related to his activities and environmental experiences.

Readiness for reading. Before a mentally retarded child can learn to read as well as his inherent capabilities will permit, he must be ready for the stage of reading development to which he is exposed. He should have attained a mental maturity commensurate with the reading task with which he is confronted. He should be forearmed with experiences and language comprehensions that will give meaning to reading content. He should be possessed of an attitude of wanting to learn to read.

Mental capacity for learning to read. A mental age of six or six and one-half years was long accepted as the minimal age at which a child could be expected to profit from formal instruction in reading. A number of recent studies have shown that many children can be taught at a much earlier mental age. One investigator of the problem suggested that it is a good idea to wait until a mentally retarded child has attained a mental age of eight years before beginning instruction in reading. The author, however, is of the opinion that there is no specific mental age that should be arbitrarily accepted as the basic age of reading readiness for all mentally retarded children. If a child has reached a mental age of six or six and one-half years but has not attained a state of readiness to learn to read, he should be made the object of special attention to locate and, if possible, correct deterring factors. When a pupil fails to respond to persistent and ordinarily effective techniques the need for remedial techniques is indicated.

Firsthand experiences are needed. The preschool experiences of a mentally retarded child can seldom be relied upon to provide him with an adequate background for beginning reading. He has probably been exposed to fewer of the needed experiences than has the average child; he has probably learned less from the experiences he has had; and he has probably shown less than average initiative in seeking out worthwhile experiences on his own. The school should provide various types of activities to compensate for, and supplement, his inadequate preschool experiences. He needs firsthand contacts with people and things. He needs to see things and handle things; he needs to go places and do things.

Developing reading readiness. To avert failure and dislike for it, reading needs to be cautiously approached. Preparatory pre-reading activities should:

Provide experiences that will give the child things to think about, talk about and later read about.

Help the child to extend his understanding and use of language.

Expose the child to books. Picture books and well-illustrated story books should be readily available for his browsing, enjoyment and conversational inspiration.

Provide opportunity to listen to reading of stories of interest.

Take part in building experience stories.

Teach the child to discriminate—to look for likenesses and differences of size, shape and patterns.

Establish in the child's mind the idea that reading is a means of communication and expression of thought, not just a word-calling process.

Create a desire to learn to read.

Testing for reading readiness. There are a number of reading readiness tests commercially available. Carefully chosen, and used with the right pupil at the right time, a readiness test may serve to confirm or deny a pupil's readiness for beginning reading. In forming judgments of a child's reading readiness the teacher may ask: Does he possess a vocabulary of sufficient size and variety? Has he had the experiences that will prepare him for the reading content with which he will come in contact? Has he acquired sufficient discriminative ability to associate spoken words with their corresponding printed patterns?

The reading vocabulary should be limited to words that already have meaning for the reader. Unfamiliar words have no place in the reading materials offered during the early learning stages of a mentally retarded reader. The words used should be those within the child's own speaking and listening vocabulary. Of course, one of the purposes of expanding experiences is to add to a child's store of language meanings, but the reading of any newly acquired words should be preceded by their conversational usage.

Use of reading readiness workbooks. After a child has had numerous and varied experiences with things and activities natural to his environment, reading readiness workbooks may often be introduced to his learning advantage. The pictures should be of things familiar to the child, things he has encountered in his home, school, neighborhood, or play life. The exercises of these books are usually designed to help a child become increasingly discriminative and to observe increasingly more refined details, until he has reached a point where he can detect likenesses and differences in printed words.

Workbooks should be regarded as supplementary material. The teacher's judgment must be relied upon to decide whether the use of workbooks may be advantageous to a child, and when their use should be started. The teacher should not rely upon them alone to prepare a child for reading readiness. If at any time it is noted that the material is becoming too difficult for a child to easily handle, the books should be laid aside for the time being. To allow a child to arrive at a frustration point in the use of books is an effective way to start building an attitude of distaste toward books and reading. Used at the right stage of a pupil's readiness development, reading readiness books may be found helpful. The child's evidence of interest and skill in their use must be relied upon as guides.

Meaning should be stressed. Reading to understand meaning should be stressed at all stages of a pupil's reading progress. Reading in its true sense is not mere word calling. Too many retarded children can glibly recite the words on a printed page, with but little, if any, comprehension of the thoughts expressed. Rote reading, if it can be called reading, has little developmental worth for the retardate. Beyond a possible feeling of mastery over word symbols that may result from their accurate pronunciation, and a possible satisfaction derived from the belief that he has performed well in the eyes of his teacher and his classmates, rote reading is of small service to the retardate. Comprehension of meaning should always take precedence over the mere recital of printed words.

Choosing beginning readers for the retarded child. The first books used should be well illustrated, with pictures designed to clarify and give clues to the meaning of the context. The books should be short in length, with one-page stories, and with not more text on a single page than can be read in the length of time compatible with the reader's attention span. Reading a number of short books with a considerable overlapping of vocabulary is much to be preferred to repetitious use of a single primer or reader. If a book can be read with ease enough to hold the interest of the reader and if words needing further practice appear in new context even though some of the words may not be permanently fixed in his memory, more progress will be made. The number of new words introduced at any one time should be limited, and should be used over and over again in new contexts until they become a part of the child's reading vocabulary. An overburden of mechanical reading difficulties causes frustration. The child learns *to* read through reading about things with which he is already familiar; learning *from* reading may be expected only after he has built up a reading vocabulary of considerable size.

Choosing basal readers. When a pupil has reached a state of reading readiness that warrants the use of basal readers, search should be made for those with low vocabulary burdens and high levels of interest. The larger percentage of the words should be common sight words. Newly introduced sight words should be repeated often enough for a high percentage of them to become a permanent part of the pupil's reading vocabulary. The content of basic reading materials should be easy enough for the pupil to be able to read with a relatively small amount of preparation, but should also help to extend his reading vocabulary.

Supplementing the use of the basal reader. The basal reader should be well supplemented by the use of other reading materials associated with schoolroom activities. It may sometimes be found desirable to lay aside the basal reader for a day or two, and use the reading period as a preparatory period for the next page or two to come. The same characters and vocabularies may be used in additional teacher-composed stories. When return to the book is made, the pages may be facilely and satisfyingly read. This practice is helpful when the number of new words appearing on a page is more than the pupil can master during one reading period. Manuals and guidebooks for use with basal readers are usually carefully prepared and contain helpful suggestions about the teaching of reading.

Choosing materials of interest to the beginning reader of lesser ability. There are some eight to ten year old mentally retarded children whose general interests are not more advanced than that of most first graders, but this does not hold true in all cases. Certain studies of play activities indicate that play and social interests are more closely related to mental age than chronological age, but the observations of the author have led to the belief that there are many educable retarded children whose social interests are in advance of their mental ages. Some readers of first grade level are more topically interesting than others. The author recalls a boy who condemned reading materials that contained "father," "mother," and "baby," as "baby stuff." When the boy was provided with stories of the same level of difficulty about workers in the community, such as the "fireman," the "policeman," his interest and ability to read noticeably improved. A child's reading interests may often be discovered by providing a number of books and observing him as he browses through them.

The interests of the older reader. As the mentally retarded reader grows older it becomes increasingly difficult to find interesting reading materials written in comprehensible language and with a low vocabulary burden. The nearer to adulthood the educable retardate is, the wider may be the divergence between his social interests and intellectual ability. For example, the ten or eleven year old boy with a mental age of six years will probably prefer chasing or playing catch with boys nearer his own chronological age, to playing "Here we go round the mulberry bush" with first graders. The reading material he would most enjoy is that based on his more mature social interests. The girl who is beginning to be interested in homemaking projects has more mature reading needs than the girl who is still playing with dolls, and preparing and serving imaginatively concocted dishes as she plays at housekeeping.

A few days before her twelfth birthday Ruth was transferred from the third grade to a special class. On her transfer card her teacher had written "incapable of learning to read." Testing showed her reading ability to be at a primer level. She had lost all interest in trying to learn to read. Following her twelfth birthday Ruth brought to school the present her mother had given her, a child's cookbook. It was written in simple language with step-by-step directions. Ruth's teacher decided that it might be a suitable reading text—one that might recapture Ruth's interest in reading The teacher used Ruth's interest in cooking as the basis for chalkboard experience stories. Stories were written around the illustrations in the book. Ruth's cooking experiences at home were talked about and incorporated into stories. Her mother became much interested in the project and wrote notes to the teacher which Ruth was permitted to read. The teacher used seat work devices which called for use of the book. For example, if the word "flour" had appeared in a chalkboard story, Ruth would hunt for recipes calling for the use of flour. She would write out the names of the articles, such as Cookies, Bread, etc., with her alphabet cards.

Once Ruth's interest in reading had been aroused, use was made of supplementary books to broaden her reading vocabulary. By the end of her first year in the special class Ruth had a good start on second grade reading.

Finding suitable reading materials for older readers. The teacher should make use of books and readers that have been found more adaptable to the reading needs of the slow learner. There are a number of lists of books that have been selected as being relatively more adaptable to the needs of the retarded reader. Some of these lists have been prepared with more care and understanding than others. Fortunately, an increasing number of publishers of textbooks for children are giving attention to the needs of the slow reader, and are marketing readers adapted to his needs. Appended to this chapter are a few lists of books with high-level interests and low-level vocabularies. The search for books with content of interest to the retardate, which are written in simply worded and understandable language, should be pursued by the teacher.

Additional reading materials. Use should be made of all kinds of directional, informational and practical reading materials related to the retardate's pursuits and activities:

Signs—traffic signals, street signs, transportation vehicle signs, danger notices, "for sale" and "to let" signs.

Floor directories in buildings.

Labels—on bottles, canned goods, crated and boxed articles.

Advertisements and notices—want ads, lost and found ads, commercial ads, health bulletins.

Instructions—recipes, directions for making articles, directions for playing games.

Informational items—city directories, road maps, telephone books, time tables, catalogs.

News items—important local, national, and international news items, weather forecasts, notices of events to come, store advertisements.

TV, radio, and movies—programs, previews, captions.

Word analysis for the retarded reader. The phonetic analysis of words seems to be of more help to some retarded readers than to others, even those children at about the same levels of achievement in reading. Some children seem to achieve greater independence than others in reading through the use of phonetics. It is probably better to discontinue instruction in phonetics, at least for the time being, for the pupil who seems to have derived negligible benefit after a fair trial. It is better to delay the teaching of phonetics and to depend upon sight words, than to have the pupil build up an attitude of dislike for reading. Sometimes failure to make good use of phonetics is based on poor teaching techniques. The teacher should become familiar with the modern approach to the teaching of word analysis before attempting to teach it. The teaching of phonetics should be chiefly treated as an individual problem. When and if he is ready, the pupil should be instructed in the use of phonetics and to the extent that it is helpful to him.

The comparative value of oral and silent reading. In his adulthood the retardate seldom has occasion to read aloud to others, but while he is learning to read, oral reading has a definite place. Oral recital of words seems to help in their retention. A certain amount of reading aloud for an audience, using easy material, is often a good way to hold interest in reading. In fact, oral reading for some retardates, and in some situations, never wholly loses its usefulness. For example, the young retarded woman as she reads a recipe may say as she reads, "two cups of flour," and as she measures the flour she may say, "one cup, two cups," and she is less apt to use a wrong amount than if she had read silently and said nothing. The more advanced the retardate becomes, the more silent reading he should be able to do.

The teaching of silent reading. Even in the early stages of his reading, the young retardate does some silent reading when he tags articles with their printed names or matches words and pictures, etc., but it will be a long time before silent reading will be the answer to his major reading needs. The readiness of retardates to respond to silent reading varies considerably, and some methods of teaching it seem to produce better results than others. How time should be apportioned between silent and oral reading, and what methods should be employed in its teaching, should be individually determined.

The importance of speed in reading. In teaching reading to the mentally retarded child, comprehension is a factor that should demand more consideration than speed. In actual life situations the chief concern of the retardate is to understand what he reads. Except possibly when he is trying to read something that appears on a movie or TV screen for a short space of time, or when failure to read quickly endangers his safety, the speed with which he reads will be of relatively minor importance. Probably neither his future schooling nor his future occupation will require that he read extensively. Improvement in comprehension improves speed in reading, and if the retardate is reading comprehensively, he will probably be reading with what is for him a practical rate of speed. Speed drills as such should be used only in exceptional cases.

Overly difficult reading material creates an attitude of frustration. A regrettably large percentage of mentally retarded children do not reach special classes until they have been pronounced reading failures. Many of them are pupils who have perhaps remained in the first grade for two years or more and then, because of age or size or because a rule of the school forbids the retention of a child for more than two years in any one grade, have been passed on to the second grade. Before they have reached the mental maturity necessary for learning to read, they have been forced into competition with second or third graders. They may be unsuccessfully and unhappily trying to compete with their classmates, or their efforts at learning may have diminished to a point where they count for little. Most of these frustrated readers build up attitudes of dislike, perhaps even hatred, for reading.

Re-creating a desire to learn to read. The first task of the teacher of the child who has learned to dislike reading is to re-create his desire to read. He should be shown that he has a need for reading, and that there are satisfactions to be derived from it. It should be made apparent to the child that the teacher has confidence in his ability to overcome the troublesome problems of the mechanics of reading. The smallest increment in learning should be noted and praised. The pupil should not be asked to become a member of a reading group in which the children's ages and interests are more infantile than his own. In order to give him practice in easy reading he may occasionally be asked to read to, rather than with, a younger group—to act as a teacher-replacement but not as a member of the class. All efforts should be made to free the reader from feelings of stress and strain.

Ties with previous reading experiences should be severed. The use of readers, workbooks, or specialized techniques of teaching reading, which might serve to remind a pupil of past failures, should be discontinued. The use of new reading materials and different methods of presenting materials may help to dispel some of the aversion to reading that exists in a pupil's mind. Any means that will serve to disassociate the attitude of failure from reading should be employed.

The use of the experience approach for the chronic non-reader. The use of the experience approach is one possible way to capture the interest of a chronically disinterested reader. For example, a boy who likes baseball may start a baseball notebook. He searches for clippings, books, and articles concerning the game or its better known players. He prepares records and notices concerning the games of the school or a local team. The teacher may read to and with him, and help adapt stories into readable language. The pupil first talks the story, and the teacher gives him whatever help is necessary to get it into printed form. One technique is for the teacher to type stories as they are conversationally formulated, with the pupil looking over his shoulder as words are spoken and typewritten. The typewritten story becomes a part of the pupil's notebook, and he seeks out illustrations and additional informational material to be worked over and become a part of his own book. Hobbies, excursions, special happenings, group or individual activities participated in by the learner, any real interest may be utilized as an experience approach for the pupil who has failed to find interest in, or a use for, reading.

Remedial treatment of common reading ailments. While the term "remedial" is usually applied to the procedures used to correct serious reading disabilities, even the pupil who gets along fairly well may be making errors which deter his reading progress and which should be corrected before they become habitual. The teacher should note the errors each pupil makes, and if there is a consistent pattern represented, a little remedial training will often remove a stumbling block to progress in reading. For example, the mistake of reversing the pronunciation of words as "was" and "saw" is a common error, the correction of which is important but does not require the services of a specialist. Failing to note all the letters in a word (as calling "black," "back") is an error not too difficult to correct. The teacher who has had no training in remedial reading should seek the aid of texts on the subject.

Treatment of special cases of reading disability. The child with a special reading disability, the one who in spite of per-

sistent teaching efforts is reading not at all or noticeably below
his mental level, should have the benefit of clinical diagnosis
and special teaching techniques. Referral should be made to a
reading, speech, or psychological clinic, according to which is
available. Lacking clinical aid, the teacher may need to do
some experimenting in order to help the chronically unrespon-
sive learner acquire some knowledge of reading. For example, the Fernald-Keller technique (described in Dr. Fernald's
book listed in the references at the end of this chapter) has succeeded with some nonreaders who have failed to respond to
other methods. When orthodox methods fail, the teacher is
justified in resorting to less orthodox ways of teaching. Hope
for teaching reading to the mentally retarded child of educable
degree should not be abandoned until every known means of
teaching has been tried.

Reading is not an isolated subject. Although, because of its
importance, a definite time should be allotted in the daily program for its instruction, the teaching of reading is not confined to those periods. Almost every subject and activity in the
curriculum is served by a knowledge of how to read. In connection with other subjects and activities the pupil should do
as much reading on his own as is practicable without distract-
ing attention from the project at hand or unduly delaying its
completion. When a project requires the reading of materials
containing an overabundance of new words, it is sometimes
desirable for the teacher and pupil to read together, with the
teacher reading the more difficult sentences, stopping to let the
pupil read those parts he is able to read without undue difficulty. The reading may need to be interrupted from time to
time for discussion to clarify meanings. If there are not too
many new words to be learned, the older reader may first silently read the material through by himself, listing new words
to be identified before oral reading is attempted. Often
preparatory reading for a project may be transferred to the
regular reading period. Retarded readers should not be per-

mitted to get the idea that reading is an isolated, one-period subject, but, by the use of reading in many situations, should be guided to look upon it as an asset to learning and living.

Reading expectancies. Mention has been made of factors that interfere with a retardate's attainment of his optimum in reading as failure to build an adequate experience and language background, the use of reading materials unsuited to interests or levels of ability, or failure to adapt teaching procedures to agree with the reader's rate of learning. Assuming he has not been overly hampered by deterrent factors, by the time the child is ready to leave school, the one with an IQ in the 50's should be reading up to the third grade level; the one with an IQ in the 60's up to the fourth grade level; and the one with an IQ in the 70's up to the fifth or sixth grade level. An occasional pupil of borderline intelligence may read as well as the average seventh grader. Expectancies and actual attainments will not always be in agreement, but a knowledge of what can generally be expected should be of help to the teacher in checking teaching results.

Establishing a permanent interest in reading. Many mentally retarded individuals never use reading except as forced upon them by the exigencies of situations. As far as possible the mental retardate should be led to appreciate the fact that reading has more than practical value. The educable retardate should be taught to read as well as he possibly can. The better he reads, the more he will enjoy reading. Through school experience he should be shown the social values of reading. Not only should the retardate become acquainted with the newspapers as something to be read, but if its reading is followed by discussions with teacher and classmates, he can learn that reading may be used to provide him with social satisfactions. Even though understanding is limited, and remarks are expressive of prejudicial likes and dislikes or expressed opinions are merely repetitions of remarks overheard, reading and talking about current events may help the retardate to feel that he is part of the world in which he lives. Listening to stories read aloud, or reading to others may help to make reading more a part of a retardate's life. Plenty of enjoyable reading helps to establish the habit of reading.

SUGGESTED READING

BETTS, EMMETT A.: A Handbook on Corrective Reading. Evanston, Illinois, Row, Peterson and Co.
This handbook contains suggestions for informally detecting reading levels and needs for correction. There are detailed suggestions regarding techniques to be employed for corrective purposes.

FERNALD, GRACE M.: Remedial Techniques in Basic School Subjects. Chapter IX. Application of Remedial Reading Techniques to Elementary School Education. New York, McGraw-Hill Book Co., 1943.
The procedures outlined in this chapter emphasize visual, auditory, and kinesthetic avenues of approach to the teaching of reading. It provides ideas for treating the needs of mentally retarded children who fail to respond to the more orthodox methods of teaching reading.

GRAY, WILLIAM S.: On Their Own in Reading. Chicago, Scott, Foresman and Co., 1960.
This book is concerned with the development of word perception and word analysis as aids to placing children "on their own in reading." While the book carries beyond the attainment levels of mentally retarded children, the portions pertaining to the early stages of reading progress are applicable to the needs of the mentally retarded reader.

KIRK, SAMUEL A.: Teaching Reading to Slow-Learning Children. Cambridge, Mass., Houghton Mifflin Co., The Riverside Press, 1940.
This book is written with the needs of the retarded reader definitely in mind. It discusses methods of detecting and building readiness for reading and methods of instruction. A list of low-vocabulary books arranged at grade levels of difficulty is appended.

SUGGESTED BOOKS FOR THE RETARDED READER

Published by The Garrard Press, Publishers, Champaign, Illinois:
  Reading level—Grade 1
  Interest level—Grades 1 to 4
      In the Woods
      Monkey Friends
      On the Farm
      Tommy's Pets
      Zoo Is Home

Reading level—Grade 2
Interest level—Grades 1 to 6
Folklore:
Irish Stories
Animal Stories
Folk Stories
"Why" Stories
Indian Folklore:
Lodge Stories
Navaho Stories
Pueblo Stories
Tepee Stories
Wigwam Stories
True Stories:
Horse Stories
Bear Stories
Circus Stories
Dog Stories
Elephant Stories
Lion and Tiger Stories

Reading level—Grade 3
Interest level—Grades 3 and up
Robinson Crusoe
Fairy Stories
Anderson Stories
Aesop's Stories
Robinson Stories
Famous Stories
Old World Stories
Far East Stories
Greek Stories
Gospel Stories
Bible Stories

Published by Harr Wagner Publishing Co., 600 Mission St., San Francisco 5, California:
Jim Forest Readers—interest levels extend beyond reading levels indicated.
Jim Forest and Ranger Don—Reading level, 1.7
Jim Forest and the Bandits—Reading level, 1.9
Jim Forest and the Mystery Hunter—Reading level, 2.2
Jim Forest and Dead Man's Peak—Reading level, 2.6
Jim Forest and the Flood—Reading level, 2.8
Jim Forest and Lone Wolf Gulch—Reading level, 3.1

The Deep-Sea Adventure Series—interest levels from 8 to 18 years
    The Sea Hunt—Reading level, 1.8
    Treasure Under the Sea—Reading level, 2.1
    Submarine Rescue—Reading level, 2.4
    The Pearl Divers—Reading level, 2.8
    Frogmen in Action—Reading level, 3.1

Books with reading level fourth grade—interest level Junior High
School:
    Desert Treasure
    The Mysterious Swamp Rider
    The Secret of the Lonesome Valley

Published by Row, Peterson and Company, Evanston, Illinois and Elmsford, New York:

The American Adventure Series
    Second reader level:
        Portugee Phillips
        Friday, the Arapaho Indian
        Squanto and the Pilgrims
    Third reader level:
        Pilot Jack Knight
        Alec Majors
        Chief Black Hawk
    Fourth reader level:
        Grant Marsh—Steamboat Captain
        Dan Morgan—Rifleman
        Cowboys and Cattle Trails
        Kit Carson
    Fifth reader level:
        Sabre Jet Race
        Buffalo Bill
        Wild Bill Hickock
        Davy Crockett
    Sixth reader level:
        Daniel Boone
        Fur Trappers of the Old West
        The Rush for Gold
        John Paul Jones

Published by Scott, Foresman, and Co., Chicago:

    Reading level—Grade 3
    Interest level—Middle grade
        The Boxcar Children, Warner
        Surprise Island, Warner

The Yellow House Mystery, Warner
Mystery Ranch, Warner
Mike's Mystery, Warner
The Six Robbens, Obermeyer
The Flying Trunk, adapted from Hans Christian Andersen by Jensen
Hidden Silver, Faulkner
1001 Nights, Warner
Mystery of Edison Brown, Montgomery

Reading level—Grades 4 to 6
Interest level—Upper grades

Adventures with Animals, Sandrus
Around the World in Eighty Days, adapted by Moderow
Call of the Wild, edited by Sandrus
Captains Courageous, adapted by Bunce
David Copperfield, adapted by Moderow
Eight Treasured Stores, adapted by Sandrus, Moderow, and Noyes ("A Christmas Carol," "The Legend of Sleepy Hollow," "Rip Van Winkle," "Ulysses and the Cyclops," "The Necklace," "The Golden Touch," "The Jumping Frog," "The Lady or the Tiger")
Famous Mysteries, edited by Sandrus
Huckleberry Finn, adapted by Brown
In Other Days, edited by Humphreville
Last of the Mohicans, adapted by Brown, Moderow
Lorna Doone, adapted by Jordan, Berglund, Washburne
Moby Dick, adapted by Brown
People to Remember, adapted by Moderow
The Prince and the Pauper, adapted by Bunce
Robinson Crusoe, adapted by Brown
Silas Marner, adapted by Bunce
Six Great Stories, edited by Moderow, Sandrus, Noyes, Mitchell ("Treasure Island," "The Legend of Sleepy Hollow," "Rip Van Winkle," "As You Like It," "Gareth and Lynette," "The Golden Touch")
Tom Sawyer, adapted by Berglund
Treasure Island, adapted by Moderow, Noyes, Mitchell
20,000 Leagues Under the Sea, adapted by Moderow
When Washington Danced, by Stratton, Moderow
The Years Between, adapted by Humphreville

Published by Educational Division, Reader's Digest Services, Inc., Pleas-
antville, New York:

The Reading Skill Builders: These supplementary readers contain
stories and articles adapted from Reader's Digest. The readers are
for reading levels grades 2 through 6; there are three books each
(Parts I, II, and III). For levels 7 and 8 there are two books each.
The selection in each reader covers a wide variety of interests. The
format of each reader is similar to a copy of Reader's Digest. The
reading level of each Skill Builder is indicated only by the number
of little winged horses on the front cover—two for second-grade
reading level, and so on through the sixth.

12/

Teaching Writing
to the Mentally
Retarded Child

Initial writing needs. Initially, the need that a child has for writing is as an instrument of expression and of establishing identity and ownership. Just as he likes to get a crayon in his hand and make marks, he likes also to get a pencil or crayon in his hand and scribble. Asked what he has written he will usually say that it is his name. Because he lives in a world where literacy is stressed, to be able to write his name gives a child a sense of membership in the world he knows.

Practical writing needs for the mentally retarded individual. The retardate's practical needs for writing are relatively limited. While he is in school his writing needs are directly connected with his spelling and written language needs. After he leaves school, writing his signature, filling in a few informational blanks, making memorandums, and writing a few letters will ordinarily take care of his writing needs.

When to start the instruction of writing. Before formal instruction in writing is begun, the child should have gained a degree of motor control and coordination that will enable him

104

to perform the required movements without undue stress and strain. He should be able to distinguish between the appearances of letters. More discernment of differences is required for writing than for reading. Occasionally a child will want to write a word or two for some special reason, and he should then be given whatever assistance he needs, even to the point of guiding his hand if necessary. Except as need for writing incidentally arises, its instruction should be postponed until a child can read at a high first, or beginning second, grade level. Learning to write then becomes easier and less time-consuming. Up to that time to be able to write his own name, and possibly an occasional word or phrase for the purpose of preserving interest in wanting to write, is sufficient.

Writing materials. The first tools of writing should be the chalkboard and chalk, or unglazed paper and large crayons. After a child has demonstrated that he has a fairly good idea of how letters are formed and connected and can write so that words may be recognized, he is ready for the use of large and soft leaded pencils, and unglazed paper with lines to help the child keep letters in a straight line and furnish a guide for the heights of letters. Pen and ink, if used at all, should be introduced only after the retardate has become a somewhat facile writer. With the use of ballpoint pens, even the older retardate has no great need for pen and ink.

Teaching the beginning writer. When formal instruction in writing is first begun, there is need for close supervision. Practice in erratic forms and movements should be avoided. Learning how to properly hold a writing utensil is a task in itself. The uninstructed beginner will often grasp his chalk or crayon with all fingers except the thumb. He needs to be shown how to use his thumb and first two fingers to hold his instrument of writing. He needs to be frequently checked to see that he has not reverted to his original way of holding chalk or crayon and that he is not holding it too firmly and rigidly. He should be shown that when he holds the crayon more loosely, his fingers do not get tired as quickly.

Use of chalkboard and chalk. The chalkboard is excellent for teaching beginning writing. It readily allows the pupil to see what the teacher is doing when they stand side by side, and there is no need to write and step aside for the child to see as is necessary when he is sitting in his seat. There is also ample space for the large writing preferred for the beginner. No attempt should be made to control the uniformity of the size of letters. At the early stage of writing, it is better to concentrate on visualizing and making correct letter forms, and habituating correct movements. Another advantage of the chalkboard is that corrections can be made quickly and easily without necessitating the rewriting of the entire word. Also there is less need for concentrating on posture and position when the child is standing at his work. With the use of the chalkboard there are not so many new things for the child to learn at one time.

Posture and Position. As soon as the pupil begins to sit at his desk for writing, special attention should be given to posture and position. The child should sit at a desk adjusted to his postural needs. His feet should be flat on the floor, and he should be able to sit with his head erect. In writing he will, of course, need to lean toward his desk, but his body should not be tightly forced against it. His desk top should not be so low that he has to lean way over his work, nor should it be so high that his shoulders are hunched unnaturally. The paper upon which he is writing should be placed a little to the right of the middle of the desk to allow for shifting as needed, and slanted so that the pencil points over the right shoulder. The writer's desk should be placed so that there is no light shining into his eyes and so that there is a good light falling on the part of the paper upon which words are being written. The left-handed writer should slant his paper so that his pencil points over his left shoulder.

Teaching form and movement. Various methods have been suggested for teaching writing forms and movements. The time spent in tracing sandpaper letters or tracing letters in the air would probably be spent better with crayon or pencil in hand, practicing the writing of letters. Actual recordings can be checked for errors. Lightly written letters may be used for tracing. Duplicate forms for pupil and teacher may be used. The teacher traces and writes a stroke at a time, pausing to let the pupil follow a movement at a time. Practice by tracing should be followed by copying without tracing as soon as the pupil can do so without making many errors. The child learns to write by writing, using the actual movements involved in writing, and getting the kinesthetic feel of the finger movements involved, as well as visualizing the shapes of letters.

Improvement in writing. Rather than compare one pupil's writing with another, it is better to keep samples of an individual pupil's writing and make comparisons from time to time. The pupil should also have models for examples of good penmanship. To aid him in the diagnosis of his own writing faults, the child may be given a few simple rules to follow, not as a set, but individually as needed. Following are a few rules, some of which will need to be stated in simpler language for the pupil:

1. Keep letters uniform in size.
2. Keep letters resting on the base line.
3. Keep letters that go above the line uniform in height.
4. Keep letters that go below the line uniform in length.
5. Make a's and o's round and closed.
6. Keep the spaces between letters and words uniform.
7. Keep slanted letters slanted in the same direction and parallel to each other.

The left-handed writer. It is better to let the retardate write with the hand for which he shows decided preference. It may be that a child is inherently left-handed, or it may be that some environmental factor is responsible for the inclination. To attempt to change the naturally left-handed writer to a right-handed one may result in undesirable nervous habits, possibly stuttering. Change from the habit may be expected to be a difficult and time-consuming task, time which could probably be more profitably spent otherwise. Since it is unlikely that the adult retardate will use writing extensively because there is little likelihood that it will have any vocational value for him, hand preference is of less concern to the retardate than to the individual for whom writing will have vocational or social significance. Adaptations in posture and position for the left-handed writer will need to be made.

Mirror-writing. If, as occasionally happens, the left-handed writer is also a mirror writer (that is, one who reverses the order of things and writes from right to left so that what has been written can be read easier when reflected in a mirror) corrective methods need to be applied. Mirror writing should be checked at its incipiency, before it has become an established habit which is difficult to change. Suggestions for correcting and preventing the tendency to gain a foothold are:

1. Indicate the starting point of writing by placing an x at the left margin of the page, or an x—) if the chalkboard is used.
2. Keep models to be copied before the pupil, and do not require much writing from memory until the habit has been overcome.
3. Frequently guide the child's hand to help him establish a sense of direction.

Manuscript writing. Manuscript writing is generally used with beginning writers. Its close similarity to print calls for fewer new learnings because letters look very much like those with which the child is already familiar through his reading. Letters do not have to be connected together to form words, and the formation of each letter is a task unto itself. One condition in using manuscript for the beginning mentally retarded writer is that the teacher should himself be a reasonably adept user of it.

Manuscript versus cursive writing for the mental retardate. Probably no hard and fast rule should be established regarding the type of handwriting to be taught to the mentally retarded child. The child's own preference, if he has indicated one, should receive consideration. A teacher will sometimes teach better that form for which he has a personal preference. The author's own preference is the use of manuscript writing for the beginner and then, unless the writer is especially adept in the use of manuscript writing, to change to cursive writing after a year or two. Much depends upon whether the child is just starting to write or whether he has already had some instruction before entering the special class. If a child already has a good start in writing cursively, it would be inadvisable to ask him to begin all over again with manuscript writing. Practically, some knowledge of manuscript writing is helpful to the adult when (as he often may) encountering the instruction, PLEASE PRINT PLAINLY. On the other hand he also needs to be at least able to read cursively written letters, etc.

Writing goals. The mentally retarded pupil should not be required to spend many hours on formal writing drills in an attempt to gain perfection of form. Some less able writers may require additional individual attention, but time should be spent to provide practice where it is needed, and not with isolated and repetitious drills which are generally intended to improve form, movement and speed. As his writing improves the pupil will usually gain enough speed to take care of his practical needs. Drill to attain a particular slant or a particular style has questionable value. The goal for the mentally retarded writer should be to learn to write so that what has been written may be easily read, but artistry need not be considered essential. Occasionally a child may be found who takes great pride in the quality of his handwriting, and for him handwriting represents a special talent, and he is entitled to the practice that will bring further improvement. If he can be allowed to get his writing instruction in some penmanship class in the regular grades, his enrollment will give him the opportunity to compete with regular grade pupils on a favorable basis, and may serve to gain their respect for him. Handwriting goals for the mentally retarded pupil should be determined by usefulness and practicality in relation to the time spent in learning.

13/

Teaching Spelling to the Mentally Retarded Child

Spelling needs are individual. The spelling needs of a retardate coincide with his need to express himself in writing. To be wholly effective the teaching of spelling should be chiefly individual in nature. Each pupil should have his own self-made spelling book. Unless it is of but temporary interest, when need for a word arises in a pupil's written work, it should be plainly written out for him, and he should copy it correctly into his spelling book.

Group needs. There are of course many words for which the need for learning will be shared by pupils of about the same level of language ability. These words may be connected with shared activities, or may be words chosen from spelling lists scientifically planned on the basis of their common written usefulness. Certainly the minds of mentally retarded children should not be cluttered with the spelling of words for which they will have no practical written use.

Reappearance of words in writing. Dr. Ayres discovered that nine words reappear so frequently in all writing that they represent one-fourth of our ordinary written language. It was also discovered that fifty one-syllable words make up one-half of all that is commonly written. Those words most commonly used should be given preference in spelling lists. If, before he leaves school, the retardate can be taught to use the dictionary to check on the spelling of words about which he is uncertain, so much the better, and the retardate should occasionally be permitted to do as others sometimes do—ask someone how to spell a word.

When to start teaching spelling. Before he seriously applies himself to learning how to spell, the mentally retarded child should have had considerable practice in copying and writing words. He should be gradually introduced to spelling. His name and a word or two of special interest may be spelled out for him as they are written for him to copy, and as he points to each letter he may echo his teacher's pronunciation of it. He may be able to remember some of the words that have been spelled out for him a number of times, but his experiences at this point should be thought of as springboards to spelling, and there should be no persistent checking to determine if he has learned them. The systematic teaching of spelling should be deferred until the child has acquired a sizable reading vocabulary and until he can write facilely enough so that he does not have to labor over the formation of each letter of the alphabet as he writes.

The alphabet and spelling. While learning the alphabet is not a necessity for learning to read, being able to recognize letters individually is essential to the learning of spelling. The alphabet, both in print and script, should be kept in a spot for easy reference. Drill in learning the letters of the alphabet in order has little value until the time comes to look up words in the dictionary. When that time has arrived, what at an earlier date would have required considerable time to learn, will be more quickly mastered by the pupil needing it.

The length of spelling lists. Only a few new words at a time should be added to a pupil's spelling list. From five to seven words a week are considered by some to be a good average; better spellers may learn as many as ten words a week. How many words should be added each week will depend upon differences in abilities, ages, and needs. It is not wise to introduce so many new words that there is no time left for review.

Pretesting. Drill on words already well learned is ineffectual teaching. Pretesting eliminates the need for spending time studying words already in the child's spelling vocabulary; however, words less frequently written may be forgotten. Weekly or bi-weekly pretests, including some words not before included as well as some words of review, are recommended. Words forgotten should be placed in the current spelling list for further study. The order of words should be changed each time they are reviewed and listed. Retardates who could spell words correctly when dictated in a certain order but who missed words when the order was changed, have been observed.

Introducing new spelling words. One procedure in learning to spell new words is to ask the child to look at and pronounce the word to be spelled. The teacher then repeats the word, and slowly and legibly writes it, naming each letter as he writes. Teacher and pupil then repeat the performances coordinately. Further practice is afforded when the child, as he whispers the letters softly to himself, writes the word from copy. After the pupil has copied the word enough times so that he thinks he can write without copy, he should test himself. Some teachers may object to allowing the pupil to whisper letters, but it has been the author's observation that pupils sometimes learn words more quickly with this added sensory attack. Beginning spellers will be able to do little studying by themselves, but as they gain in experiences most children can be taught to study spelling without supervision.

The place of oral spelling. The ability to spell orally is seldom exercised outside the classroom except perhaps to help another person who needs to write a word but is doubtful of its spelling; therefore greater emphasis should be placed on written spelling. The usefulness of spelling orally along with writing when a new word is being learned was mentioned in the previous paragraph. When oral spelling is used with writing and in the dictation of words, correct pronunciation and clear enunciation are essential.

Teaching words of more than one syllable. Words of more than one syllable should be looked at by the speller, pronounced first as a word, and then pronounced and spelled orally, syllable by syllable. The copy he has before him should have the word without syllabication followed by the syllabicated word. He should of course write it as it should naturally be written, as an undivided word. The purpose of dividing it into syllables is to make it easier to learn to spell, and not to teach how to syllabize.

Avoid practice in the erratic spelling of words. When a child is composing some bit of writing, and comes to a word he does not know how to spell, its spelling should be supplied for him eliminating guesswork. Once he has written a word a certain way, he may continue to write that way even after attention has been called to his error. Unless the pupil can write facilely and will not need to labor over the letter formations of words dictated to him, the written words should be placed before him to copy so that he will be less distracted from his problems of composition. If the word is one he probably will use again it should be placed in his regular spelling list. When words are dictated for pretesting purposes, the pupil should be instructed not to write a word unless he is quite sure he knows how to spell it. He can be told to draw a line to indicate a word's omission. When conversational periods are used to prepare for later written work, key words may be written on the chalkboard to use as spelling references when needed.

Words with special difficulties. When introducing new spelling words it is sometimes helpful to call attention to parts of words that may cause difficulty. Parts that frequently cause confusion are *al* and *le, ie* and *ei, ent* and *ant, able* and *ible,* and *ence* and *ance.* Attention may be called to the *i* before the *e* in a word, or a line drawn under the *a* or the *e* which may be substituted one for the other. The learning of rules, such as "*i* before *e* except after *c*," is not recommended.

Using words from reading as spelling words. Provided that they are words which the pupil is using in his oral and written language work, words from his reading of the day may be included in his spelling list. Encountering words in his reader and very soon after in his spelling provides multiple responses and facilitates learning; however, to place words in his spelling list only because they appear in his reading, without regard to their written usefulness, serves no real purpose.

SUGGESTED READING

FITZGERALD, JAMES A.: A Basic Life Spelling Vocabulary. Milwaukee, Wisconsin, Bruce Publishing Company, 1951.
This guide helps the teacher to formulate practical spelling lists and choose words that will be relatively more useful to the retardate throughout his life.

14/

Teaching Arithmetic to the Mentally Retarded Child

Arithmetic needs of the retardate. Since the arithmetical needs of the mentally retarded individual are relatively simple, and since the time required for teaching the fewer-than-average needed number facts is long, it is certainly not justifiable to crowd nonessential facts of arithmetic into his curriculum. The needs of the average retardate will be confined to buying and selling and money-handling situations, and a certain amount of measurement. The most imperative needs should be considered first, and the teaching of arithmetic should not extend beyond the pupil's present and probable ultimate needs.

Understanding the purpose of number. It is not uncommon to find a mentally retarded child who has acquired considerable skill in adding, subtracting, multiplying and dividing, yet who is unable to solve problems involving these same processes. Given a problem which can be solved by multiplication, the child is apt to add or subtract, or to divide if the numbers appear easily divisible. This is particularly true where much time has been devoted to practice in the use of the mechanics of number, and little to problem solving. To understand that arithmetic has purposes and is not just another classroom exercise, a pupil must have opportunities to use it in practical ways.

Processes and problem solving should be taught concurrently. Concurrent with the teaching of mechanical processes, problems, the solutions of which depend upon mechanical processes, should be used. For example, at the same time that the multiplication table of 5's is being taught, its use should be made apparent by solving problems as finding the cost of five candy bars at 5 cents a piece, or determining how many quarts of milk the milkman leaves for school lunches each week by multiplying the number of quarts used daily by the number of days in the school week. As each fact in addition, subtraction, multiplication and division is taught, it should be accompanied by use of the fact in solving problems.

Numbers and school activities should be connected. As need for the use of numbers in a school activity arises, the occasion should be used to emphasize the usefulness of numbers. Learning is facilitated when the problem involved may be used as the starting point in the teaching of some new fact. If processes are too difficult to be learned at the time, the problem may be worked out by the teacher gathering whatever help he can from the pupils. Follow-up work will depend upon pupil readiness. The closer the teaching of needed arithmetical facts can be linked with the experiences and present needs of a retarded pupil, the more likelihood there is that the child will make use of arithmetic in the solution of his out-of-school problems.

Teaching arithmetic is a step-by-step process. The number of steps involved in the teaching of the fundamentals of arithmetic are numerous. New knowledges should be introduced only as fast as they can be assimilated. Of course there will be some concurrent learnings taking place as the pupil goes along, but one step at a time is the general rule in teaching arithmetic to retarded pupils. When a pupil's errors indicate that facts have not been thoroughly learned, practice should be resumed in the unlearned facts. Allowing a pupil to become entrapped in a maze of partially learned facts is to be avoided. Often it will be found that ignorance of some single process may be the cause of lack of progress.

Unnecessary errors should be avoided. Far too many pupils get obstructive practice in arithmetical errors. An error once made is an error that may be repeated until it becomes a habit. There are many commonplace errors which may be anticipated and avoided. For example, when a pupil first begins to add two-place numbers he often adds from left to right. Direction should be given when he first starts; he may be told that when we write we go "this way," but when we add we go the "other way." Unless precautions are taken, trouble with the use of zero may be expected. The pupil should be taught that the sum of any number and zero is that number, and that zero times any number is zero. Any new fact should be carefully presented and explained to the pupil in a manner most likely to avert error. When error appears, immediate practice in the correct form should be provided. Anticipating common errors in arithmetical computations and quickly correcting errors will save much time and promote progress in arithmetic.

Counting. Numbers enter early into the life of most children, and that many of them enjoy counting is evidenced by their frequent use of it in play, rhythms, and games. Many children, upon entrance into a special class, are able to count, some children more than others. Many can count at great length in rote manner long before they have any realization of the fact that the purpose of counting is to find out how many. Even when objects are used, the young mental retardate may not coordinate his handling of the objects with his counting. His counting may need to be carefully checked for accuracy.

The importance of giving meaning to counting. The young retardate should be taught early that one counts not just for the exercise of counting, but because he has need of it in his daily life. He should count concrete objects more often than merely reciting numbers so that he may learn their right order.

He should have frequent opportunity to use counting in life situations. He can count out the right number of paper cups in which to serve milk to the class. He can count sheets of paper, crayons, and other articles that need to be passed to the class. He can count pennies to pay for something at the toy grocery store.

Counting accompanied by physical activity. Combining counting with a physical activity provides a pleasant change from just sitting and counting objects—walking and counting steps as he walks; walking and touching chairs, desks, or children as he counts; counting as he claps his hands or tries to touch the floor with his hands. If motions are synchronized with counting, a rhythm of performance, that often seems to help in learning to count, may be established.

The written or printed number. To associate the written or printed symbol of a number with its already known numerical value represents another teaching step. Neither the spoken word *five* nor a group of five objects is automatically associated in the mind of a retarded child with the written word or printed symbol 5. Definite effort is required before the association becomes automatic. Posters with a number of like pictured objects accompanied by the appropriate written and printed symbols may be used as guides to counting out the right number of blocks or other small objects. The pictured objects and the concrete objects should be varied so that the child will not get the mistaken idea that the number symbols are associated only with certain objects.

Learning to write numbers. The correct way to write numbers should be demonstrated to the child. Attempting to teach how to write numbers by tracing them is usually ineffective. Just to place the number before the child to be copied without supervision or guidance is almost certain to result in unconventional ways of writing numbers. More than one child has been observed making an *8* by placing one circle on the top of another. Until correct movements have been learned, teacher and pupil should perform together, with the pupil following the teacher move by move. Unsupervised practice may then follow.

Counting, as a tool, has its limitations. Even after a mentally retarded individual has become a part of a community, there is not much need for him to know how to count into the thousands. He can be taught that the more digits there are, the larger the number is. He can be taught to tell which is the larger of two numbers having the same number of digits. With the exception of locating pages in a book or locating street addresses, a mentally retarded person will probably have little need to use large ordinal numbers. To be able to locate a house numbered 7850 does not require that a person be able to count to that number without error. The use of telephone numbers merely calls for their recital in proper order. Practice in learning to count should be limited by its usefulness to the individual.

Arithmetic textbooks for the mentally retarded. It is not practical to depend upon arithmetic textbooks prepared for primary and elementary school pupils as day-by-day guides for the mentally retarded pupil. While sometimes fundamentals already mastered will appear more often than is needed for practice, it is more likely that there will be insufficient provision for practice in needed facts. Children vary greatly in their need for practice. Often there are problems included which bear no relationship to the retarded child's experiences or his ability to understand. Generally much of the language used is beyond the retarded child's ability to understand. The teacher may find a certain amount of guidance in an arithmetic textbook—suggestions on the ways to present certain phases of arithmetic, and problems which she may reword and simplify in complexity—but the textbook has little value in the hands of the pupil himself.

Arithmetical terms and symbols. So many signs and terms may be used to express the same thing in arithmetic, that the retarded child has difficulty in keeping them all in mind or associating them properly. Because the confusion of terms and symbols impedes the progress of the mentally retarded pupil, only the really necessary and most commonly used ones should be employed. It is suggested that a reference chart in which like terms and symbols are linked together be made available for ready reference. To illustrate: Multiply — Times — X.

Use of drill cards. Drill cards for the simple addition and subtraction combinations, for the multiplication tables through 12, and for the corresponding tables of division are suggested. They are helpful teaching devices if properly used. There is sometimes a tendency to waste time and effort by giving practice and repractice in already well-learned combinations. If used to give practice where it is needed and to supplement, not supplant, the teaching of arithmetic in problematical situations, drill cards may be used to learning advantage. To avoid teaching in isolation, the relationship between drill and problem solving must be established for the pupil. Selecting a card from a drill pack and using it in connection with the solution of a problem at hand is one suggested way to help pupils understand the purpose of drill.

Problems should be presented as simply as possible. Arithmetic problems should be presented to the retarded pupil in a way that helps him concentrate on the problem as a problem and helps him find the answer as quickly and easily as he can. The wording of the problem should be as brief as is consistent with understanding. Words not already a part of the pupil's reading vocabulary should be avoided. His thinking should not be blocked by the "intrusion of irrelevant linguistic difficulties." As much oral presentation of problems as is necessary to clarify meanings for pupils should be used. A few oral instructions will often reduce considerably the amount of reading required, and then to furnish individual pupils lists of articles to be purchased, and to ask them to find the total cost of each list is a good simplifying device. Pictures of articles of merchandise with prices attached may be useful with pupils of limited reading vocabularies.

The teaching of arithmetic should be kept as pleasurable as possible. When a situation demands the use of numbers, and the retardate is able to answer his needs by the application of known numerical facts and processes, the success of his accomplishment will ordinarily furnish him with sufficient satisfaction for his efforts. The use of numbers in game situations is a commonly used incentive for learning number facts. The use of numbers may be incidental to playing the game itself, or counting and adding may be required for scorekeeping, or the play spirit may be used to provide incentive for learning number facts. The amount of time devoted to arithmetic games should be determined by the amount of arithmetical learning taking place.

Reduce the amount of number copying. While correctness of solution rather than speed of performance should be the goal in teaching arithmetic to the retarded child, the more automatic elemental arithmetical responses become, the more quickly and accurately solutions may be arrived at. The retardate's responses will generally be slower than average, but elemental combinations will need to be used comparatively facilely if problems of greater complexity are to be solved accurately. One of the hindrances to speed in problem solving is the amount of figure copying that is often required. Sometimes the pupil gets so involved in getting numbers correctly set down that he loses sight of the problem involved. Until he has learned to respond with reasonable rapidity to simple problems as adding 8 and 2 or multiplying 2 by 6, he will learn to solve these same problems more quickly if he is required to do less copying. If, instead of being required to both copy and solve problems, the pupil is furnished with sets of problems to which he need add only the answers, he can accomplish more in less time; he can concentrate on finding right answers without becoming entangled in a mesh of figure copying. If the practice gained is not enough to furnish needed improvement in writing numbers, he can be instructed to first set down all his problems correctly and, after they have been checked for accuracy and legibility, he can go back and center his attention on solving and setting down the right answers.

Problem solving. What is said in the previous paragraph applies chiefly to the learning of the mechanics of numbers. In problem situations, where the pupil must figure out for himself which process or processes should be employed to get correct results, the pupil will need to set down the figures needed—he needs to know what to do when the teacher is not there to help him. If a pupil has difficulty in knowing which process to apply in which situation, a number of problems calling for the application of different processes may be orally presented to him, and without taking time to work problems through to their completion, he may be asked to tell whether to add, subtract, multiply, or divide. As soon as he can respond with a reasonable percentage of right responses, written work may be begun or resumed.

Setting down a problem. While pupils should be taught to set down problems with moderate neatness, making figures that can be easily read and that are properly aligned, standards should not be emphasized beyond the point of usefulness. The important thing is to get the right result in a reasonable length of time. To write down whatever is necessary to the solution of a problem is all that should be required. For example, a pupil has been asked to place chairs in an assembly room for a meeting of his own and two other classes, with a half-dozen extra chairs for the teachers and a possible visitor or two. If he has been told that he must always indicate what it is that he is adding, his actions will be greatly hampered. There are 12 children in his own room, 20 in another, and 24 in the other. Should he write 20 chairs, or 20 children? What words should he put down for the extra chairs? How should he indicate which rooms the children come from? The only problem really involved is adding, 20, 24, 12 and 6; he knows what to do after he gets the answer, 62. Requiring the retardate to write down a lot of explanatory words only impedes his thinking and interferes with his finding the right results as quickly as possible. The pupil might better be getting more practice in finding results.

Learning to tell time. Time enters into the daily life of

everyone. The average entrant into a special class will have a feeling of need to be able to tell time, his learning how to do so is necessarily a gradual process. First, he should be taught the position of the long and short hands as they are at the full hours. After he is consistently able to tell when it is one o'clock, two o'clock, and so on, he may be taught the use of the long hand to show how many minutes it is before or after the hour. Finally the use of the terms *half past*, a *quarter to*, and a *quarter after* may be taught. A discarded clock, with Arabic numbers and hands that may be turned at will, is an excellent aid in teaching how to tell time. It takes long association and much explanation before the calendar becomes a useful instrument to the retarded child. Calendars should be kept in the room, and dates of individual or class interest should be circled. Questions relating to time should be frequently asked, and checked on the calendar. When did it, or when will it, happen? How long ago was that? After a pupil has gained some time knowledges, they should be reviewed so that he may be taught whatever additional facts he needs to know. Some of his learnings will need to be molded into systematic forms. For example, he may know the present month, know his birthday month, know what month Christmas comes, but he may need to be taught the order of the months of the year.

The use of money. Application of arithmetical knowledges to the use of money is a practical necessity for any mentally retarded individual who ever has any money to spend. Each pupil needs to be fortified with as much useful knowledge as he is capable of learning to protect him against fraud and error. Even though he may not be a wise spender and purchases made may not represent value received, he should at least know what money to offer in payment and whether or not he is given correct change when change is due. He should be taught to make change in the commercially approved manner, as a problem in addition and not as one in subtraction. Making change should be generally treated as an oral problem, in accordance with life situations where, every time he makes change, he cannot sit down with pencil and paper and figure out the answer.

Classroom opportunities for learning how to use money. Because of its major importance to the individual, some type of activity involving money should be in daily progress in the special classroom, as playing store. For the younger child articles should be priced at a penny or two, a nickel or a dime, but as soon as a pupil has reached a point where he can appreciate differences in values, prices used should agree with actual current prices. Situations may be varied according to the needs and interests of participating pupils. Some projects allied to teaching the uses of money are: making out sales slips, keeping personal or school accounts, and making simple budgets. The pupil cannot receive too much practice in the handling of money in situations analogous to those he will encounter in real life.

Use of monetary signs. The retardate will need to know the meaning of the signs ¢ and $, as well as the use of the decimal point to distinguish between dollar and cents. The usual order of learning is first the ¢, and then the $, and later, if his comprehension permits, the use of the dollar sign together with the decimal point. Pupils should be specifically instructed that cents are always placed to the right of the decimal point, and dollars to the left, and that when the number of cents is less than ten, a zero should be placed before the number. Practice should be given in the recognition and use of these forms before they are included in written problems.

Teaching the value of money. While no amount of training may be expected to turn a retardate into a consistently wise spender of money, he may be taught a measure of thrift and given some idea of the relative values of purchasable articles. Even though price tags do not represent true values, the young retardate may be taught to shop around to get the most satisfaction out of his few pennies. Unless the rules of the school forbid their use, catalogs, newspaper ads, and handbills may be used to good teaching advantage. If lunches are prepared and served by special class pupils, practical experience in planning, buying, and accounting may be afforded. For retardates who will become active members of a community as the time approaches when they will be leaving school, the use of sham checks, in amounts which might represent weekly incomes, may be endorsed, cashed, budgeted and spent. Regularly depositing a certain amount of his imaginary earnings into an imaginary savings account, watching the amount grow, and withdrawing only for worthwhile purposes cannot be expected to prevent the retardate from becoming a member of the "buy now, pay later" group of citizens, but it may inculcate the idea of saving a portion of today's earnings for tomorrow's needs. The simulated situation should be replaced by the real situation when and where possible. The older pupil who may be a part-time earner should have his pay checks discussed realistically. He should learn the meaning of budgeting, withholding taxes, overtime payments, and the like.

The teaching of measurements. The teaching of tables of measurements to the retardate has little value as compared to the time consumed in learning them. Observation has been made of retarded children who were able to recite a number of tables of measurement, yet who were unable to make use of them in figuring amounts, sizes, distances or time. The retarded pupil should be taught such common measurements as will be most useful to him not through the memorizing of tables, but through repeated use of measuring devices. The special classroom should be equipped with foot rules, yard sticks, scales, measuring cups, and pint, quart, and gallon containers, and whatever other measuring devices may be of service to him. The best way for the retardate to learn how to measure is by measuring.

Teaching fractions to the retardate. Such fractions as are taught to the retardate should be in association with practical situations. A child gives half of his candy bar to his playmate. A game is to be played where half the class is seated and the other half stands up. How many chairs will be needed? Most of the use for fractions will be in connection with the measurement of things. The use of recipes calls for some use of fractions—to measure correct amounts of ingredients or to cut down recipes according to the number of people to be served. In his use of linear measurement he may need to know the meaning of an inch and three-fourths, or a foot and a half, etc. Whatever is taught about fractions should be taught through practical associations and use. It is generally unwise to spend time trying to teach addition, subtraction, multiplication and division of fractions even to the more educable retardate.

Reviewing and testing in arithmetic. The use of standardized achievement tests was discussed in Chapter 4. Teacher-made tests will be needed to supplement the occasional use of standardized tests. Often when teaching emphasis has been centered on a particular arithmetical process for some time, it will be found that lapses in use of other processes have caused the child to forget. Need for review is indicated, and tests which include problems involving a number of processes, mixed in the order of their presentation so that a pupil's arithmetical comprehensions may be tested, should be given.

Summarization. As far as is practicable, arithmetic for retardates should be taught in the situations where need for it arises. When a need exceeds the retardate's ability to perform or when the steps involved are too numerous or too dependent upon other unlearned steps, such use of the situation should be made as is apt to increase a pupil's appreciation of the value of knowledge about number facts. Simulated situations will often be needed to support actual situations if essential arithmetical facts are to be thoroughly learned. The mechanics of numbers should be as pleasurably taught as possible, and the use of learned facts should be made apparent to the pupil by linking them to meaningful situations. Practice should be given only where practice is needed, and practice in errors should be avoided. The educable retardate might be taught certain numerical facts; but unless they bear relationship to the child's present or future needs, the facts are better left untaught, and the time that might be used in their learning may be spent more purposively.

SUGGESTED READING

GROSSNICKLE, FOSTER E., and BRUECKNER, LEO J.: Discovering Meanings in Arithmetic. Philadelphia, The John C. Winston Co., 1959.
The authors of this book are specific in their explanations of how to teach the mechanics of numbers. Concrete methods of presenting number facts in meaningful situations are well presented.

15/

Teaching Social Studies to the Mentally Retarded Child

Objectives in the teaching of social studies to the mentally retarded child. The retardate should be taught facts about the world he lives in and the people who inhabit it, and for which he may have practical or social value. The primary aim should be to instill within him a respectful attitude toward school, city, state and nation, and a feeling of tolerance toward people in general. He should learn that he has a duty not only to safeguard his own health and well being, but that he also has a share in the responsibility of promoting and protecting the welfare of others. He should store up a few geographical and historical facts that are common matters of knowledge.

The approach to social studies should be on a local level. Geography as often taught requires that a pupil live through experiences remote in distance and character from everyday life. History requires that a pupil transport himself into the past. Understanding depends upon imagination. Whatever the retardate eventually comes to understand about remote times and places will depend upon his fund of knowledges of the here-and-now, on which his less facile imagination can draw for comparison. He should first be taught how to get about independently in his own environment, and how to make it useful to himself. It cannot be expected that a retardate will always live in the same community, but there will usually be enough similarity in environmental conditions so that considerable transfer of training will result. What little the retardate learns about the people of yesterday will be in comparison with the people of today. Learning the names of all the countries of Europe and their capitals and the dates of many of the battles fought during the Revolutionary War may be a possible attainment for a retardate but, having learned them, neither his own nor the welfare of those about him will have been much enhanced.

Social studies and the home. A young retardate may enter school with meager knowledges about his home and the people in it. If he is deficient in these knowledges, the school should teach him those things he has not learned as a member of a family. He should know:

Something about the composition of his family—the number of people in it, and their relationship to himself and each other.

Something about the type of home in which he lives—the number of rooms, the material of which it is made, etc.

The names of the different rooms and their uses.

How his home is lighted.

How his home is heated.

What cooking facilities there are.

Location of his home by street and number.

The telephone number if there is a telephone in the home.

The occupations or household duties of different family members.

The child should also assume some home duties if home cooperation permits. If he is not already performing some simple home tasks, the school should endeavor to prepare him for the assumption of one or more simple chores.

Social studies and the school. As a member of a class in school, sharing rights and privileges with others, the retardate is in a natural community situation where he may be taught habits of good citizenship. He should learn to:

Have respect for property by learning to care for his own, and also respect the property rights of others.

Assume his share of the care of the schoolroom which is his daytime home.

Have pride in the appearance of the school building and the school grounds.

Know and observe the general rules governing school and playground.

Know that good conduct, while journeying between home and school, is a part of his obligation as a good citizen.

Social studies and the neighborhood.

While the retardate is learning his role as an acceptable school citizen, he should be guided in explorations of his neighborhood. He should:

Establish contacts with places of interest and usefulness to him—stores and markets, library, museum, church of his faith, recreation centers, parks, firehouse, police headquarters, homes of friends and relatives, etc.

Learn convenient modes of transportation to and from places he wants to go.

Have opportunity to meet and know some of the people of his neighborhood—the policeman on the corner, the tradesman, the health or social worker, the director of the recreation center, etc.

Be taught to observe notices posted in public places for the convenience and instruction of visitors.

Have opportunity to take excursions so that he can be taught to observe traffic signs and rules for pedestrians.

Be taught from whom to ask information when it is needed. Discussions before excursions will help the retardate to courteously and pertinently ask for information.

Have opportunity to learn from his classmates through conversational pooling of experiences. For example, a pupil went to the Y.M.C.A. swimming pool with his brother. He tells his class what he and his brother did, and what he saw others doing. He tells where the Y.M.C.A. is located, and how to get there.

Occupational geography.

The retardate can acquire some idea of the interdependence of people by learning about different types of employment within his community. Possible ap-

proaches to the study of occupational geography are: making
a list of, and discussing, the occupations of members of the
families of the pupils; visiting places of employment; and learning about articles of usefulness from their origins, through
manufacturing and sales stages to the users, or starting with
the user and back to their origins. Even more emphasis should
be placed upon the part that workers play than to manufacturing processes employed. Whatever approach is used should
be linked to the pupil and his needs, and planned to help him
understand how others contribute to his welfare and happiness.
For older pupils, thought should be given to possibilities of
their future employment. What kind of jobs does the community offer? What are the requirements? How would a pupil
go about trying to get a particular job? Where and how would
a pupil gather information about possible employment? As suggested earlier, the pupils should have practice in filling out
forms required of them as applicants for work.

Modes of travel. The retardate will find useful a knowledge
of different ways of traveling—automobile, bus, elevated lines,
subways, trains, boats, airplanes, etc. Some knowledge about
routes of travel, passenger and cargo services, and speeds of
travel also may be useful to many retardates. What cargoes
are carried? Who guides and services the vehicles?

Approach to knowledges about faraway places. Knowledge
about faraway places is secondary in importance to knowledge
about the retardate's more immediate environment. The geographical knowledges about places beyond the retardate's own
locale that should be taught are those that come naturally and
easily. The most natural approach to the study of geography is
through the study of people, through stories and pictures of
Dutch, Japanese, or other persons. The locations of places,
descriptions of physical aspects of a country, climates, in-
dustries, names of political divisions, etc., will have little meaning for the mentally retarded child except in their relationship
to people. How do the people dress? How is their dress influenced by the climate? What kind of homes do they live in?

Does what they do to earn a livelihood bear any relationship to the physical aspects of the country? How would one get there? Where the retardate travels imaginatively, and how far he travels, should largely be controlled by his manifest interests.

History for the retardate. The formal study of history has no place in the curriculum of the retardate. Historical facts about people and events may be presented best through story form. Dramatization, if not overemployed, may help to give meaning to certain historical happenings. Dramatization should not be permitted to consume more time than the worth of learning warrants. In evaluating the usefulness of the dramatization of historical events, however, consideration should be given to possible concomitant values—increased language usage, establishment of self-confidence, respect gained by other pupils in the school who may view a production, or other social or intellectual value.

Training for obedience of the law. Unless retardates are subjected to undue outside influences, their habits of respect for the law acquired as pupils in a special class may be expected to be carried over into adult life. These habits should include those of honesty, respect for property rights, and readiness to conform to rules and regulations adopted in the interest of public welfare. There are rules and ordinances peculiar to a retardate's locale which need to be specifically brought to his attention if he is not to become a legal offender. He should be familiar with traffic rules for pedestrians in his area. If there is a probability that he will become a driver of a vehicle, he should be taught the meanings of traffic signs and road markings, and learn the rules for driving before he leaves school. There may be laws of trespass with which he should become acquainted. If he is a bicycle rider he should know the rules that apply to him as a rider. Local regulations regarding the disposal of garbage, forbidding the keeping of animals within the city limits, or other health regulations which might apply to him have curricular importance.

Use of public services. The retardate should be taught how to use public services designed for his protection and convenience:

Police protection—The retardate should learn to look upon policemen as friends, as persons to whom he may turn in time of trouble. As far as can be done without creating an unhealthy interest in disorder and crime, the retardate should be instructed in the proper times to call for police help.

Fire protection—The retardate should be taught how to report fires, use fire alarms, acquire the habit of looking for fire exits, leave fire hydrants alone, and perform during fire drills.

Use of mails—The retardate should learn about postage rates for letters, how to properly wrap and mail parcel post packages, should visit a post office to learn where to mail different types of mail, learn how to send money orders, etc.

Use of the public library—The retardate should learn about the services of the library through visits to the library, having his own library card, etc.

Use of the telephone—The retardate should be taught how to make local and long distance telephone calls, how to use a telephone directory, and some of the courtesies expected of a telephone user.

Obtaining licenses—The retardate should be taught how and where to obtain licenses he may need—driver's, fishing or hunting, vendor's, etc.

The retardate and taxes. The retardate may learn, in a very general way, some of the purposes of taxation by pointing out a few of the apparent ways in which public money is spent —to pay the mayor, the president or other public officials known to the pupil, and to pay for schools, roads, or other familiar usages. He should know that, if he is employed, he is expected to fill out an income tax form whether or not he is obliged to pay taxes. Even with the best instruction the adult retardate should have someone wiser than himself to advise him in tax matters that affect him, and he should be taught where to seek such help if help is not provided through his family.

The retardate and employment. Apart from technical instruction he may receive, the employable retardate should be equipped with as much information as the school can give him about the best ways of seeking and obtaining employment. The writing of applications and the proper filling out of forms has been discussed previously. The retardate should also have knowledge of agencies in his community which are concerned with employment and employment problems. Figuring out what the cost is when he employs the services of a private employment agency may be included as a part of his practical training.

Introducing the use of maps. The purpose of maps will probably be best understood by the retardate if their use is first applied to his own local area. A good start is to use a map, drawn to scale, centered around the location of the school, covering an area of about half a square mile and indicating the location of two or three known places, as a child's home, a grocery store, and the firehouse. A test of the child's ability to use the map is whether or not he is able to indicate the location of other well-known places. As a pupil shows readiness, areas on the map may be extended, and the scales that are used may be modified to fit needs. To begin the use of maps by asking a child to draw to scale maps of the schoolyard or other small familiar area, consumes a lot of time and is of relatively little usefulness to him.

Knowledges that are of social value to the retardate. As suggested early in this chapter, the retardate should store up some commonplace facts of geography and history. There are persons, places, and events of yesterday as well as today that crop up so frequently in conversations that to be totally uninformed about them brands an individual as illiterate in the eyes of his fellows. There are calendar dates that may be used as natural teaching approaches for some of this informational data—Lincoln's birthday, Washington's birthday, the Fourth of July, Columbus day, Armistice day, Thanksgiving, and Christmas. The names of local public officials, the governor of the state, and the President of the United States of America are among those which should bring a look of recognition to the face of the retardate who desires membership in a social group of adults.

SUGGESTED SOCIAL STUDY READERS

Published by Harr Wagner Publishing Co., 600 Mission Street, San Francisco, California:

Girls and Boys at Home—Reading level Grade 1

Girls and Boys at School—Reading level Grade 2

Days' River Farm—Reading level Grades 2 or 3

Foods from Far and Near—Reading level Grades 2 or 3

American Heroes—Reading level Intermediate Grades:

Real Adventures with Discoverers of America (Lief Ericson, Columbus, Magellan, Ponce de Leon)

Real Adventures with the Pilgrim Settlers (William Bradford, Miles Standish, Roger Williams, Squanto)

Real Adventures with American Patriots (Washington, Jefferson, Ethan Allen, John Paul Jones)

Real Adventures with American Pathfinders (Daniel Boone, Lewis & Clark, Zebulon Pike, Davey Crockett)

Real Adventure with American Plainsmen (Kit Carson, Wild Bill Hickok, Custer, Buffalo Bill)

Published by Row, Peterson and Company, Evanston, Illinois and Elmsford, New York:

The American Adventure Series (See page 101.)

Film-Story Books—Grade levels Intermediate to Junior High School:

Chinese Children

French Children

Italian Children

Japanese Children

Norwegian Children

Spanish Children

16/

Teaching Manual Arts to the Mentally Retarded Child

The manual abilities of the retardate. It is sometimes claimed that mental retardates tend to exceed in their manual abilities to compensate for their lesser intellectual abilities. It is probably more accurate to say that many educable retardates more nearly approach the norms in motor abilities than in intellectual abilities. There may be physical reasons why a mental retardate is not able to perform well manually, but retardates are more "thing-minded" than "thought-minded"; they are "better able to deal with things than with ideas." The mental retardate is frequently a much better master of manual than of academic tools.

The manual training needs of the mentally retarded pupil. Upon entrance to a special class the mentally retarded child is usually in need of some type of manual training to help him establish better manual control, as well as to furnish him with a means of expressing himself. During the intermediate years of the retardate's school life is the time when, in addition to the satisfaction of educational needs, manual training should begin to disclose a pupil's aptitudes or inaptitudes for more particularized types of manual training. The final two or three years of the retardate's school life should be slanted vocationally if aptitudes warrant and if training facilities are available. Whatever the trainable degree of manual dexterity a mentally retarded child possesses should be recognized and developed in accordance with its present and forseeable usefulness to him. Even though the specific job he may eventually have may not require the exact skills he has learned at school, some transfer of training may be expected, and the pupil will learn the new task more readily than if he had received no training at all. If he has had much practice in the use of his hands, he will more quickly find how to use them in a new manual situation.

Teaching manual arts to the mentally retarded child during his earlier school years. Manual work for the younger mentally retarded child should favor the use of the larger muscles. The projects chosen should not require a long time for their completion. It is not wise to insist on perfection in workmanship as long as the child shows interest and improves in his work. Work which calls for lengthy, formal instructions should be avoided. Processes and skills should be taught not as something apart, but in connection with purposeful projects.

Purposeful projects requiring handwork. When a child makes something because he has a particular use for it in mind, his interest in making the article will usually be increased. Below are a few illustrations of purposeful activities involving the use of handwork:

> Mary brings a doll to school, and the topic of conversation becomes dolls and their needs, or a friend of the class presents it with a doll: Pupils cut and make doll clothes; dress and undress dolls; launder doll clothes; make a doll house and furniture; make bedding for the doll's bed.

> Johnny loses a button off his shirt: Children learn how to sew buttons on their clothing.

> Christmas is coming: Decorations for the Christmas tree are made; gifts are made for relatives and friends.

Valentine's day is near: Children make valentines for each other and for their friends.

A school exhibit is to be held: The pupils make suitable articles showing the different types of handwork they can do.

Members of the class are learning to read: Pre-primer booklets are illustrated with drawings or cut-out pictures; phrases chosen from reading lessons are illustrated with drawings or cuttings; silent reading lessons requiring handwork may be used.

The members of a primary special class are invited to take part in a school assembly: They help with the making of their costumes; they make some of the properties for their dramatization.

The schoolroom needs to be refurbished: The pupils paint the chairs; they paint the sandtable and refill it with clean sand; they paint the flower box which the older boys have made for them; they decorate flower pots and plant seeds; they decorate containers for bulbs and start them; they make bookends for the reading table; they make bright posters for the room.

Pupils have been losing and mixing up their rubbers: They make bags with their names on to keep them in.

SAFETY FIRST needs to be emphasized: The pupils make booklets to illustrate matters of safety about which they have been talking; they make miniature safety devices to use in safety drills and dramatizations.

Objectives in teaching manual arts to older pupils. After pupils have attained a certain amount of manual dexterity, training for practical usefulness as well as for self-expression deserves more consideration. Mentally retarded individuals differ widely in their manual abilities, but the pupil with average or better-than-average ability should receive instruction that will increase his competency as a householder by teaching him how to keep his home in repair and how to improve his home environment. He should receive instruction that will improve his chances as a job-seeker. Incidentally, if they manifest interest, girls as well as boys should be permitted instruction in woodworking, and other manual arts.

Teaching the care of tools. The user of tools should be taught how to care for them. Each tool should have its place, and the pupil should be taught to put tools back when he is through with them. He should be taught to keep tools in a dry place and to grease them occasionally to prevent rusting.

Some skills to be taught. Some of the ordinary and commonly used skills that a retardate will find useful, and that need to be taught carefully are:

Sawing:

Use rip saws to cut with the grain.
Use cross saws to cut across the grain.
Use coping saws for sawing curves.

Planing:

In planing keep the cutter set so that a thin shaving can be cut.

Nailing:

Be sure the right kind of nail is selected for the place in which it is to be used.
When driving nails into small or thin pieces of wood, first use an awl or drill to drive a hole slightly longer than the nail. In nailing one piece to another, the worker should stand so that he may sight along the second piece into which he is nailing.
If a nail takes the wrong direction, withdraw it and start in a new location; do not strike it sidewise as this only bends the nail.
When withdrawing a nail, place a block of wood under the hood of the hammer to prevent marring the wood.

Filing:

File diagonally, not straight, across the edge.
Use flat files on flat and convex surfaces.
Use round files on concave surfaces.

Using sandpaper:

Wrap a piece of sandpaper around a block of wood, and use this to rub the part you wish to get smooth.
Always sandpaper with the grain.
To sandpaper the edges, place the sandpaper on a smooth, flat place and draw the wood over it.

Painting:

Let color dry before another coat is applied.
Let the colors join on sharp definite lines.
Pick up only a small amount of color with the brush.
Lay colors on with a thin coat.
Thin oil paints with turpentine, not with shellac.
When not in use, keep oil paint brushes suspended in turpentine to prevent them from becoming stiff.
To clean oil brushes, use turpentine; then wash the brushes thoroughly in yellow soap and water, and rinse out lather before using, or use a commercial cleaner and follow the manufacturer's directions.

Staining or shellacking:

All surfaces should be carefully sanded before shellacking.
Careful sanding after each shellacking makes a fine, smooth surface.
Let one coat dry before applying another.
Thin shellac with wood alcohol.
Mix only turpentine with turpentine stain.
Shellac brushes should be suspended in shellac when not in use.
Clean brushes thoroughly before putting away.

Some miscellaneous hints. Whenever practicable, use a contrivance, as a vise or handscrew, to hold work in place, leaving both hands free to do better work. Measurements should be laid off with the ruler held upon its edges. To avoid splitting when using boring tools, set the work upon a flat surface of soft wood; or, as soon as the point of the spur projects, turn and bore from the opposite side. When fastening with screws, a hole should be bored through the upper piece to receive the screw.

Who shall teach manual arts to the mentally retarded? Those phases of the manual arts which involve the use of skilled techniques should be taught by skilled technicians. It is highly desirable that older retardates, who can be trained for specific vocations, have the opportunity to be taught by those familiar with the ins and outs of the tasks involved. Many special class teachers learn enough about woodworking, painting, weaving, or other of the manual arts to be able to instruct pupils under their care. Many units of activity within the special classroom call for at least a minimum knowledge of the manual arts. However, when a pupil has passed the primary stage of the learning of the manual arts, he should be taught to perform in the workmanlike manner of an adult worker. Persons who have been trained as teachers of the mentally retarded will usually have had some instruction in the manual arts included in their training. The teacher should not attempt to teach any type of manual arts unless he is reasonably well qualified to teach it.

The following two books are suggested for the teacher who has had no specific training in the manual arts. The teacher who has pupils below the age of need for specific vocational training, should find the books of help in instruction connected with handwork and construction problems growing out of units of activity:

MOORE, FRANK C., ET AL.: Handicrafts for Elementary Schools: A Handbook of Practical Suggestions for Teachers. Washington, D. C., Heath and Co., 1953.

TAYLOR, JEANNE: Child's Book of Carpentry. Philadelphia, Chilton Co., 1948.

The following books are for teachers who wish to instruct pupils in one or more of the types of handicraft indicated:

ATWATER, M. M.: Byways in Handweaving. New York, Macmillan Company, 1954.

MILLER, JOSEPHINE V.: Paper Sculpture and Construction. Peoria, Illinois, Charles A. Bennett Company, 1957.

PERRY, L. D.: Bird Houses. Peoria, Illinois, Charles A. Bennett Company, 1955.

SHIRLEY, A. J.: Handicraft in Metal. Philadelphia, Lippincott, 1953.

HOOPER, RODNEY: Plastics for the Home Craftsman. Philadelphia, Lippincott, 1953.

17/

Teaching Household Arts to the Mentally Retarded Child

The need for knowledge of the household arts. Many girls in classes for the mentally retarded will become housewives and mothers. Some of them will serve as domestics. Those capable of learning should be taught to do plain cooking, to darn and mend, to do practical sewing, to do laundry work, to keep a house in presentable condition, and to expend household money as wisely as they can.

Homemaking projects should be practical. Projects chosen for instruction in homemaking should be directly related to the daily lives of pupils. The way for mentally retarded pupils to learn to cook, sew, and keep house is through practice in the skills involved. Practice gained by making things for themselves, their homes, or the school has a greater chance of resulting in permanently useful habits than practice gained through formal assignments. A seam on a doll's dress or a hem for a towel has far more value than the same bit of sewing on a detached piece of cloth. A little practice beforehand, however, is sometimes useful if a project is already underway, and the pupil knows where the stitch being practiced is to be used. *The method of teaching household arts.* Much of the work in sewing, cooking, and housekeeping should be taught by demonstration methods. It is better to have a pupil learn a new stitch in sewing needed for the completion of a sewing project by having the teacher show a pupil how, and letting the pupil try it with coarse materials, than to instruct by lessons on the chalkboard or by use of pictures and instruction sheets. It is desirable that a pupil learn how to use printed recipes in cooking but, in the beginning, demonstration should go along with the reading of the recipe. If noon lunches are served, pupils should be responsible for as much of their preparation as possible. If there is a school cafeteria pupils should be allowed to serve in any capacity for which they are equipped.

Care of the schoolroom. Although the cleaning of the floors and other general cleaning jobs are the responsibility of the school custodian, there are still many household duties that may be assumed by the pupils. Below are some of the tasks for which they may be held responsible:

Use a door mat.

Clean the chalkboard.

Dust articles of furniture, window sills, shelves, low-hung pictures, etc.

Observe orderly methods of disposing of waste materials.

Sharpen and distribute pencils.

Take care of plants, window boxes, etc.

Keep the library table or shelf neat.

Keep display tables in good order.

Keep the cloakroom orderly; each child should have his own locker or hook or place on a rack; coats should be kept on hangers if possible; rubbers should be kept in bags or in some manner to prevent their getting mixed up or coming in contact with clothing.

Keep closets, cupboards, drawers, and other storage spaces neat and orderly.

Wash glass doors, windows, and mirrors when needed.

Keep sinks and washbowls clean.

Housekeeping knowledges to be taught before leaving school. Before the mentally retarded girl, or the boy if he shows interest, leaves the special class, he or she should have acquired as many of the following knowledges as possible:

Care of floors and woodwork:
    Sweeping floors.
    Washing floors.
    Vacuuming floors and rugs.
    Waxing floors.
    Care of linoleum and plastic floorings.
    Care of tiled surfaces.
    Dusting woodwork.
    Cleaning painted woodwork and walls.
    Cleaning varnished woodwork.

Care of furniture:
    Dusting furniture.
    Use of furniture polishes and waxes.
    Care of upholstered furniture.

Care of kitchen:
    Care of sink.
    Care of kitchen utensils.
    Care of small electrical kitchen appliances, such as food mixers and toasters.
    Care of cupboards.
    Care of refrigerator.
    Care of stoves.
    Care of floors and woodwork.
    Care of furniture.

Care of bathroom:
    Keep well ventilated.
    Daily care.
    Weekly care.
    Care of bath tubs and wash bowls.
    Care of toilet bowl.
    Care of floors.
    Washing bath mats and rugs.
    Putting toilet articles away.
    Changing towels.
    Keeping bathroom from becoming cluttered with soiled clothes or clothing that belongs in other places.

Care of bedroom:
    Changing bed linens.
    Changing and cleaning mattresses.
    Making beds.

Care of floors and furniture.
Keeping drawers in chests and bureaus in order.
Keeping unused bedding clean and properly stored.
Care of clothes closets.

Miscellaneous household tasks:
Washing windows.
Care of window curtains.
Changing table linens, towels, etc. as needed.
Sanitary garbage disposal.
Care of basement.
Care of closets and storage places.
Preventing and controlling infestations by household pests through the use of insecticides, traps, etc.

Laundering:
Using hampers or other suitable places for soiled clothes.
Sorting clothes for washing.
Removing stains.
Setting colors in new materials.
Learning to properly use and care for washing machines.
Learning to properly hang clothes on clotheslines, as many will not possess dryers.
Learning to properly wash and dry drip-dry materials.
Folding and sprinkling clothes that need it.
Ironing different types of clothes and materials.

Safety in the home. It is important that the retarded individual be taught rules of safety within the home. The proper methods of the safe use of small electrical appliances should be emphasized—the proper way to remove plugs from sockets, the dangers from frayed electrical cords, the danger to young children from disconnected cords left in wall sockets, the importance of keeping radios away from sinks and bath tubs. Among the many safety subjects that should be included are: the importance of turning handles on pots and pans to minimize the danger of spilling hot foods or water, and the chance of accidents from toys or articles left on steps. Lists of the common dangers within the home are readily available.

Teaching some facts about child care. Since many mentally retarded girls will become mothers after leaving school and many others will have some responsibility for the care of children, it is essential that they be taught to care for children as well as they can. The teacher will find the use of a good manual on infant hygiene and child training helpful. Use can be made of the information regarded as most pertinent to the needs of the pupils. Language may be simplified, and subject matter may be correlated with language and reading along with as much practical demonstration as facilities permit. A baby manikin is often used to help in the teaching of the proper holding, bathing and care of a baby. The health habits of a growing child are proper subject matter, including learning about the amounts and kinds of sleep, food, rest, and exercise that a growing child needs.

Activity unit on child care. It is suggested that all older girls who may eventually have any responsibility for the care and training of children should have the opportunity for actual contacts with children and child situations. Proper foods should be discussed and prepared. Practice with manikins has previously been suggested. Visits to store departments which cater to children's needs may be followed by discussions about essential clothing and furnishings. Keeping expenses down by the use of home-manufactured and satisfactory available substitutes should be demonstrated. Arrangements may be made for visits to supervised play situations in nursery schools or kindergartens, followed by discussions of the methods employed by those in charge to encourage good behavior and the types of correction or discipline employed when necessary. Periods of observation should be reinforced by increased opportunities for assuming responsibility for the care and training of children.

Fifteen year old Elizabeth was often kept home from the special class which she attended to baby-sit with a toddler age sister. The class was receiving instruction in child care. Consent was obtained from the mother and other necessary authorities to have the child brought to school every afternoon. Duties for the toddler's physical care and play supervision were divided among individual pupils, with an exchange of responsibilities from time to time to provide needed practice. The school nurse gave help and advice as needed. Through her, necessary medical attention was provided. The class received instruction and experience in child care, the baby benefited from the attention and care she received, and the older sister was able to remain in school.

Cookery for the mental retardate. Since future employment as cooks in diners or as cafeteria helpers is a possibility
for them, mentally retarded girls, and boys who show interest,
should be taught as much as they can learn and use profitably
on the selection and preparation of food. While first attention
should be given to the preparation of simple and wholesome
foods, it is the occasional baking of a birthday cake or the
preparation of a fancier-than-usual dish for a special occasion
that gives zest and adds interest to cookery even though a pupil
may not be able to perform more than one or two of the steps
involved. Most pupils will need to act as cook's helpers, learning a step at a time, before they are ready to undertake the
preparation of a dish by themselves; the preparation of an
entire meal takes place later.

The preparation of food. Ways of cooking food should be
discussed while the food is actually prepared according to one
of the following methods: boiling, roasting, frying, broiling,
poaching, baking. The relative merits of the different methods
may be discussed with respect to the kind of food being prepared, the amount of time involved, the amount of heat necessary, and the effects of the different methods upon palatability
and digestibility.

The care of food. The prospective young housekeeper should
be taught how to care for food. She should be taught:

To cover food before putting it away.

To use air-tight containers for coffee, tea, or foods which lose flavor
through exposure to air.

To know which foods require refrigeration.

Not to leave milk, cream, or other foods which spoil quickly outside
of the refrigerator longer than necessary.

To keep vegetable bins well ventilated and in a cool, dry place,
and not to allow decayed vegetables to accumulate in them.

To protect against and exterminate insects and rodents.

Marketing for food. Some aspects of marketing can be
taught in connection with arithmetic and the use of the school
store. Occasional visits to markets, supplemented by the study

and use of newspaper ads and advertising sheets, are of much help. The actual buying of supplies for use in classroom cookery and the preparation of school lunches are practical applications of problems in marketing. Suggested topics for discussion and demonstration are: comparative shopping; advantages and disadvantages of buying certain items in quantities; watching for special sales on food staples; buying seasonal food items when they are most plentiful and least expensive.

Planning menus. Daily menus should be planned around simple, nourishing, and easily prepared foods. Rather than discussing carbohydrates, fats and proteins, the mentally retarded pupil will be better able to prepare well-balanced meals if given a few simple rules to follow and given practice in writing typical menus, which provide variety in diet as well as body needs. A few suggested rules are:

Some food each day from each of the following groups:

Group 1. Sweet foods—those containing sugar, honey, molasses or syrup. Starch foods—those made from flour or cereals, macaroni, spaghetti, noodles, etc.

Group 2. Fatty foods—fat on meats, butter, oleomargarine, cream, oils, etc.

Group 3. Body building foods—lean meat, fish, fowl, eggs, milk, cheese, beans, peas, etc.

Plenty of milk each day, either to drink or used in the preparation of other foods.

Meat, eggs, fish, fowl, or cheese at least twice a day.

At least two vegetables other than potatoes each day.

A leafy green vegetable every day.

Fruit or fruit juice every day.

Some teachers may wish to modify this list of suggestions, but whatever instructions are given should be as specific as possible.

General instructions in the preparation of a meal. Before the mentally retarded girl will be ready to prepare an entire meal, she will need to have learned a number of individual tasks. If she is to have a meal ready and on the table on time she may need to use a schedule which has been planned and written out.

After some practice she may be able to carry plans in her mind. A few general suggestions for making schedules are:

Have the menu clearly in mind or written out if necessary.

Learn to prepare things beforehand during less busy moments— casseroles to be slipped into the oven, sugar bowls filled, butter on a plate ready to be put on the table, salad greens washed and ready to cut up, etc.

Study recipes beforehand.

Get materials and utensils together before starting the preparation for cooking or baking.

Plan the setting of the table so that it will be done before a meal is ready to be put on the table—before cooking is started, or when waiting for something to finish cooking.

Have in mind a list of tasks that cannot be done until the last moment so that they can be quickly accomplished.

Having everything prepared and on the table at the proper time comes only through planning and experience; before she leaves school the girl should be given as much practice as possible in planning and in the execution of plans.

After-meal care. In addition to how to prepare a meal, the mentally retarded girl should be taught what to do after the meal is over. Some specific tasks are:

Soaking dishes—Cooking utensils, and serving dishes that need it, should be put to soak as soon after food is removed as possible.

Putting food away—Milk, butter, or other food needing refrigeration, and bread or other foods that may dry out should be put away immediately following the meal.

Dishes should be rinsed if necessary, and stacked in a place near the washing center.

Proper washing, rinsing and drying of dishes should be taught, as many will not have mechanical dishwashers in their homes.

Cleaning silver and caring for chromium pieces.

Scouring utensils that need it.

Care of sink.

Disposal of garbage.

Cleaning top of stove and wiping out oven if needed.

Washing dish towels if needed; always allowing towels to dry before putting in hamper.

Keeping wearing apparel in good condition. The mentally retarded future homemaker should be taught how to care for family wearing apparel. She should be taught to do as many of the following jobs as she can:

To put clothes away neatly in drawers or closets.

To brush clothes that need it before putting away after wearing.

To remove spots and stains from clothing.

To press clothes carefully, using a pressing cloth and moisture when needed, and adjusting the heat of the iron to do the best pressing job.

Be able to tell the difference between washable clothing and that which requires dry cleaning.

Look at labels which give directions for washing. (It is not recommended that the retardate be encouraged to do dry cleaning in the home because of the dangers involved if directions are not explicitly followed.)

Protect woolens against moths.

Clean shoes and rubbers before putting away.

Keep shoes polished, or cleaned by the method best suited for the material of which they are made.

Sew on buttons.

Mend tears and holes in the manner best suited to repair the damage.

Sewing for the mentally retarded girl. It is more important that a girl be able to properly take care of garments, than know how to make them. Sewing, however, has practical value for the girl with an aptitude for it, and it may develop into a very fine hobby. The girl who has learned to sew a good seam or make a good hem, while making doll clothing or hemming towels for home or school, is then ready to undertake more complicated sewing tasks, as making aprons or other equally difficult sewing projects.

Sewing projects for the more capable pupil. The use of the sewing machine should not be undertaken until the young seamstress can be trusted to use it with the caution necessary to protect her against accidents. The use of patterns is only for better sewers. Some patterns are much easier to use than others; only those that are easiest to lay on materials and cut out properly, and have simple directions, should be used. Here again, demonstration should accompany the use of patterns until the pupil understands the meaning of the various directions and markings. It is recommended that the same brand of pattern be used for most sewing projects, because directions vary from one make to another. Patterns cut along simple lines should be given preference. Except for those pupils who are exceptionally adept and have considerable experience, the use of patterns with inset pleats, peculiar shaped pieces, etc., should be avoided.

Homemaking projects should consider individual needs. In choosing homemaking tasks to be taught to a mental retardate, consideration should be given to the type of home wherein the knowledges learned will be applied. Instruction should be for the purpose of helping the pupil to maintain the best standards of homemaking her aptitudes will permit. Because of time limitations and individual differences in aptitudes, choices in subject matter will often need to be made. If a girl is not good at sewing, she should be taught how to buy and care for clothing best suited to her needs, instead of trying to teach her to make dresses. If a pupil has no flair for cooking, teaching should be confined to the preparation of foods which require little skill. There should be concentration on a few dishes which may be in most demand by the retardate's family and which will provide a reasonably healthful diet.

18/

Learning Through Experience

Avoid teaching in isolation. A fact that is taught in isolation not only takes longer to be learned, but also is more apt to be forgotten. The same fact taught in a situation where it is of use to a pupil, where it helps him find the answer to some current problem, where its applicability and usefulness is apparent, may be learned more quickly and remembered longer. Having used the knowledge once in a meaningful way, he will be apt to use it voluntarily when need for it arises again.

Giving meaning to drill. As emphasized elsewhere in this book considerable repetition is needed for the fixation of facts in the memory of the retardate, but drill will be more effective when the child can be helped to see the relation to situations where the repeated facts apply. For example, a new word is being taught in reading. The word may be taught solely by monotonous, repetitious drill, or it can be related to reading situations which involve thought and meaning. The word can be located on the printed page, it can be used in written language, and the printed version may be brought to view when the word is brought up in conversation. Generally speaking, the need to read the word should precede drill on its recognition. In like manner, the child may be shown the need for drill in arithmetical combinations, addition, subtraction, multiplication and the like. When the pupil understands that drill is for the purpose of helping him to remember useful facts because he has experienced the need for them, then drill may become something more than an exercise in mental gymnastics.

Various names have been applied to methods of choosing subject matter and motivating learning. The ways and means of getting children to learn more things of more worth have been variously labeled. Some years ago educators, recognizing the various points at which school subjects touched upon each other, began to talk about the correlation of subjects. Subject matter was still the starting point for teaching. Later, attention was directed to the importance of starting with an encountered situation or need, and then introducing subject matter where it helped and applied to the solution of problems involved. Educators generally agree that learning is facilitated when a child can see some use for that which he is attempting to learn. Whether or not our efforts to teach realistically are labeled as group activities, projects, or experience units makes little difference as long as chosen teaching vehicles utilize the environment of the mentally retarded pupil to give meaning to, and make learning easier in, areas of importance to his living, and add to his practical or social growth and development.

Activities may vary in size and scope. A situation may arise which affords an opportunity for learning by one person or for a group. An activity may be of short duration as related to a need of the moment, or it may provide continuous new learnings for a long period of time. A unit of activity may be concerned primarily with one field of knowledge or branch of learning, or it may include in its scope different categories of knowledge, coordinating them in a way to help pupils understand and appreciate the relationships between certain things in life. An unplanned and natural occurrence may initiate the need for learning certain facts and knowledges; or an experience may be planned and arranged to bring pupils in contact with, and afford them the opportunity to learn, things of importance to them, an importance sometimes initially more apparent to the teacher than to the pupil.

Goals should be kept in mind. Sometimes teachers believe that every school subject should be related in some manner to a major project, or that every suggested lead should be followed. Such connections as are natural and helpful to the completion of a project should be utilized, but there should be no attempt to force a connection where one does not naturally exist. Trying to follow every lead, or implied lead, that arises in connection with a project is quite apt to distract attention from the main purposes and goals. Concomitant learnings are important, but they should never be permitted to lead a learner down paths which are so long and devious that they cause him to lose his sense of direction.

An illustration of failure to adhere to goals. A group of retarded pupils, who were nearing an age when they would have imperative needs for handling money, embarked on a storekeeping unit of activity. They watched the store ads, and placed current prices on their make-believe wares. They took turns as storekeeper and customers. They had barely started with their important buying, selling and change-making problems when the teacher, thinking she should tie in their activities with geography, began to divert the attention of the pupils by questions. From what country does the coffee you are selling come? The bananas? etc. Transportation problems were introduced and discussed. Booklets, which required a great deal of time, were made. The store was soon forgotten as a place of business where pupils could learn how to use their money wisely, where they could learn how to carry out money transactions without being shortchanged or shortchanging others. Long before the store project had served its major purpose—sufficient practice to permit practical phases of the handling of money to become habitual—the attention of the pupils was directed elsewhere.

Evaluating a group activity. When considering suggestions for a suitable unit of activity, and before selecting one, the teacher should be convinced of the relationship of the activity to the environment and experiences of the members of the participating group, its relationship to their needs and interests, and the probable usefulness of the knowledges, skills, habits and attitudes that may be expected to be derived. An activity should be simple enough in character to assure its successful completion, but sufficiently difficult to present a challenge to learning.

Criteria for evaluating a unit of activity. A well-selected unit of activity should:

Be within reach of successful completion.

Reach beyond that already achieved.

Solicit and hold the interest of the pupils participating.

Involve knowledges, habits, and skills sufficiently worthwhile learning to justify the expenditure of time involved.

Find the teacher relatively less and the pupils relatively more in the foreground as the project proceeds.

Tentative planning. Plans should be discussed before actual work is begun on a project. Pupil help should be used as much as possible to gather useful materials and references that will assure an auspicious start. While the pupils should be permitted as much choice as possible, guidance may be needed to weed out unneeded and unrelated materials which may serve only to confuse and delay the advancement of the project. While ultimate goals should be kept in mind, plans for reaching the goals should remain flexible. Planning will need to be a step-by-step process, with the outcomes of one step indicating what the next step should be.

Record of progress. Records of progress made by pupils while working upon units of activity should be kept. Mentally retarded pupils like to see written down statements about how well they are doing in their work; records are acknowledgments of accomplishments. A notation about a child's individual contribution to a project, placed on the bulletin board where all can see, is an incentive to further effort. A group record may be some type of chart which records facts and skills learned, activities or projects accomplished, and dates to indicate speed of progress. The keeping of individual charts is applicable to some types of projects. A special place may be assigned for displaying charts and graphs. If there is insufficient space to exhibit all individual records at one time, the records may be rotated until each child's has been shown. The teacher's judgment must be relied upon in choosing the best forms for recording individual and collective accomplishments. Choice will be influenced by the amount of time involved in making charts and graphs, the ages of the pupils who will interpret them, and the nature and length of the activities represented. The record which best helps both teacher and pupils to evaluate progress made should be selected for use.

Summarizations of units of activity should be kept. After a unit of activity has been completed, the teacher should make a summarized account of the project. The final summary should include:

1. How the activity originated.
2. The chief goal or goals.
3. Books and references used.
4. Other materials used and where obtained.
5. Group outcomes—academic and social.
6. Individual outcomes—academic and personal habits and attitudes acquired.
7. Possible suggestions for follow-up projects.

SUGGESTED READING

MARTENS, ELISE H.: Group Activities for Mentally Retarded Children. Department of Interior, Bulletin No. 11. Washington, D. C., United States Government Printing Office, 1936.
This is a compilation of group activities that were contributed by teachers in special classes for mentally retarded children.

STRICKLAND, RUTH G.: How to Build a Work Unit. Bulletin No. 5. Washington, D. C., Federal Security Agency, United States Office of Education, 1946.
This pamphlet indicates the procedures to be followed in planning and building a unit of work.

19/

Teaching the Mentally Retarded Child the Use of Leisure

The responsibility of the school for training for leisure.
How the mentally retarded person uses his leisure time when
not at school or vocationally occupied has much to do with his
state of well-being and stability of behavior. It is during his
moments and hours of leisure that he is most apt to get in
trouble. The school has a responsibility of helping the retardate learn how to use his leisure wisely and satisfyingly.

The retarded child needs to learn how to play with others.
The special class has to accept the child as he is upon entrance.
His play habits should be scrutinized, and he should be placed
in a play group where there is reasonable expectation of his
acceptance as a playfellow, or, if he is not yet ready for acceptance in any group, he should be taught those things and ways
that will prepare him for acceptance. He needs to be taught
the meaning of fair play, and to accept and abide by the rules
of the game. He needs to be taught to accept defeat without
resentment. His best play placement is with a group where the
demands made upon him are in accordance with his ability to

respond properly, and where he will have a chance to become more mature in his play habits.

School provisions for practice in the use of leisure. The special classroom should be equipped with play materials suited to the ages and play needs of the pupils. Equipment for the physical activities of younger pupils and games and materials for older pupils should be provided. There should be some class-owned equipment—a ball and bat, jumping ropes, a soft ball, and other simple equipment that may be used in the gymnasium or on the playground. There should be a game shelf with picture puzzles, solitaire games, and games that may be played quietly by two or more players. There should be games that are perennial pastimes, and some that are currently popular. A choice of games may be the reward for industrious effort that merits a few minutes of leisurely relaxation. The game shelf is a convenience when pupils are kept indoors during recess or at the lunch period because of inclement weather. In short, the school should familiarize a pupil with games and play materials, and give him a chance to know how to use them.

Music for the retardate. Whatever musical abilities the retardate possesses should be utilized. The school cannot be expected to furnish expensive musical instruments or pay instructional fees for private lessons, but it can commend and encourage the efforts of parents who may be providing musical instruction for children with a passable degree of musical talent. In one instance a pupil was disturbed because he had to discontinue his piano instruction. The family home and its furnishings had burned, and the parents could not afford to replace the boy's piano immediately. The boy was permitted to continue his practice, using the schoolroom piano after school hours. In some instances mentally retarded individuals have been able to perform sufficiently well to become members of school bands or orchestras. There have been instances reported where retardates have been employed in community bands. The assistance of a music instructor in the school sometimes may be obtained to help retarded pupils, with trainable amounts of musical ability, receive the instruction they need.

Musical activities in the special class. Rhythmic bands furnish pleasure and training for mentally retarded pupils. If simple and easily manipulated instruments are used, instruction may be started at a fairly early age. A certain amount of individual instruction and practice may be needed before a pupil is ready to perform harmoniously with a group of players. How well a pupil responds to the use of certain toy instruments may be the clue to his interest in the use of a specific type of real musical instrument. Harmonicas and kazoos are popular instruments with special class pupils. Even pupils of relatively low IQ's have been taught to play bugles and use the drums fairly well. After they had preliminary instruction in how to blow a bugle and how to handle drum sticks, they learned simple tunes by observing and listening to the instructor play, and then practicing along with him.

Singing for the retardate. Singing is a universally employed leisure time activity. Most mentally retarded children can be taught to sing well enough so that they can join in group singing without discord. Generally, in the special classroom, singing should be taught imitatively, rather than by trying to teach pupils to read music. Usually, following and imitating the teacher and a few leaders will be all that is needed to get children to "follow the tune." It is sometimes a good idea to hum and sing "la la" to a tune before trying to fit the words to it. The occasional child who sings in a monotone may need some scale work, and trying to sing scales as they are played on the piano is helpful. With the help of a teacher who likes music, most children can learn to sing "by ear." The chief use of books should be to supply lyrics. It is only the more talented singer who will profit from vocal lessons as such. Part singing is for advanced singers only.

Selections of songs to sing. The songs used with singing games make good selections for younger singers. Folk songs have a general appeal. Currently popular songs, unless for some good reason they are considered unsuitable, may be brought into the schoolroom. The songs are particularly helpful to the pupil who is trying to ally himself with a social group in which the songs are sung. The national anthem, of course, and a few other widely sung patriotic songs should be a part of the retarded pupil's repertoire.

Rhythmic activities for the retardate. The retarded child should begin his training in rhythm as early as possible. An ability to respond more or less rhythmically to music may open up avenues of leisure time pastimes—rhythmic games, folk dancing, and social dancing. If rhythmic training does no more than help a child move less awkwardly than he would otherwise, he may become a less conspicuous individual, and be able to fit more comfortably in certain social and leisure time situations.

Drawing and painting for the beginner. Drawing and painting are enjoyed by many mentally retarded children as a means of self-expression. Finger painting or painting on large sheets of paper with large brushes is a good start. Crayons should be thick and not easily broken. At first the child should be allowed to scribble or daub, and be encouraged to talk about what he has done without too much interrogation. The child should be permitted to take the initiative in talking, and he should know that he has a willing listener. If the child is garbed in a smock and provided with rags or sponges, powder paints and tempera are good media. The beginner's techniques should not be a matter of concern.

Drawing and painting for the older pupil. Pupils who continue to be interested in drawing and painting, after they have experimented with them as instruments of self-expression, should be encouraged to develop whatever artistic abilities they have. Murals are excellent cooperative art projects, with individuals working on separate sheets which are then joined together. After pupils have been helped to discover how different materials and media may be used effectively, the further use of materials should be largely a matter of choice. Whatever talent is exposed should have opportunity for development. The retardate who likes to draw or paint pictures, no matter how crude, should be furnished with the supplies to carry on his hobby. The child with enough creative ability to draw or paint pictures that win the commendation of others will derive increased satisfaction. Occasionally a retardate will be able to copy, with considerable skill, the works of other artists.

Establishing hobby interests for the retardate. The retardate with a hobby interest has an asset of great worth. The school should make a definite effort to introduce the retardate to hobbies which may carry over into his adult life. Handwork of some type is often the answer to filling leisure hours. Whether the hobby is "weaving, basket making, leather tooling, woodworking, sewing, embroidering, or some current handwork fad makes little difference as long as the retardate enjoys doing it . . . Whether the hobby be making or growing something, collecting something, developing some talent, developing some physical prowess, participating in some type of sports, or whatever, is of little importance as long as it holds the interests and efforts of the participator."*

Leisure time reading. The newsstands are plentifully supplied with mawkishly and sordidly written books and magazines of romance and adventure. Because of the simplicity of the language in which they are written, the undesirable books and magazines readily fall into the hands of retarded readers. The school should do what it can to establish more healthful reading interests for its older pupils. The better pictorial magazines and even well-selected comic books deserve a place on the reading table in a special classroom. Interest in comics often carries over into the adulthood of those who feel that reading is an irksome task instead of a pleasure. The retarded child who seems to get enjoyment from comics should be introduced to the nonharmful variety, avoiding those which should be on the prohibited list for all children. The retarded pupil should learn how to use the library, and become acquainted with the librarians who can help him in finding books of his liking—stories of simple romance, wholesome adventure, out-

---

* Slaughter, Stella S.: The Mentally Retarded Child and His Parent. New York, Harper and Brothers, 1960, p. 110.

door life, or any topic that captures his interest. Although the retardate may be expected to be more a doer than a reader, whatever healthful reading interests he has should be preserved and perpetuated. However, the retardate who displays interest only in the more undesirable types of reading should have his attentions directed as much as possible toward more active pursuits.

Solitary use of leisure. Individuals do not constantly live in gregarious situations, and retardates should be taught how to make use of their time when not in the company of others. Reading is, of course, a solitary occupation; some hobbies require no cooperative effort. Working jigsaw puzzles, playing games of solitaire, or practicing physical stunts may serve as pastimes. The retardate who has some constructive pastimes with which he may occupy himself is less apt to display delinquency or other undesirable behavior than a retardate who has none.

Outdoor activities. The school should introduce the retardate to pleasurable outdoor activities. Games of the outdoor variety may be introduced on the playground. Hiking, picnicking, etc., may be enjoyed by the class; the children discover the fun to be had, and learn to take care of themselves out-of-doors.

Using leisure to improve surroundings. The school should do whatever it can to create a sense of pride in the physical aspects of the retardate's surroundings. Opportunity for the child to have a part in keeping the schoolroom and the school building and grounds attractive and orderly is a step toward building that pride. Learning to make, and being allowed to take home, articles which add to the attractiveness of the home, and learning to make simple home repairs, are among the projects which may help to develop a pride in the appearance of the home. The retardate who has developed such a pride will naturally use some of his leisure in satisfying that pride.

A home improvement project. A group of older retardates carried on a competitive project planned to improve the appearances of their homes and yards. The teacher offered a prize for the pupil who did the most to improve his home and surroundings during his out-of-school hours. The principal of the school, the president of the school P.T.A., and the manual training instructor were appointed to judge the contest. They inspected the premises involved at the beginning of the contest and then again on its final day. The project was started on the first day of April, and the day for judging was just before the close of school. Yards were raked and mowed, gardens were planted, window boxes were made, steps were repaired, fences were painted, etc. At the picnic day celebration on the last day of school, the grand prize was awarded the winner, and each child who participated received a smaller prize for his efforts.

The recreational opportunities of the neighborhood. Through inquiry from pupils and others, the teacher may find out what games and activities are popular with recreational and social groups of the neighborhood in which a pupil lives. Practice may be provided to better equip the pupil to fit in a group which he may desire to join. His performance may be improved so that he will find ready acceptance as a member of the group.

Knowledge of community recreational opportunities. The retardate who will soon be leaving school should receive information about places in his community where healthful recreational opportunities may be found. Assuming he is qualified for admission, effort should be made to assist him in gaining entrance to those places, or to help him join those organizations in which he expresses interest.

Finding right leisure time companions. Where and with whom the retardate spends his leisure time is of more importance than the activities involved. The retardate is more apt to find suitable companionship in a Y.M.C.A. or Y.W.C.A. or in a well-supervised church or community recreational center, than he is in a public pool hall. The neighborhood coffee gathering or fun club is less apt to turn up questionable acquaintances than is the tavern or bar. The formation of social and hobby clubs, while pupils are still enrolled in school, may serve as a nucleus for later clubs of like nature. Before the retardate leaves school, he should be helped to establish a few worthwhile friendships and desirable social contacts.

SUGGESTED BOOKS

CROWNINSHIELD, ETHEL: The Sing and Play Book. Boston, Boston Music Co., 1941.
This book contains music for rhythms, dancing, and singing. It has many of the old favorites, as "Rig a Jig Jig" and "Old MacDonald."

HARTLEY, RUTH E., AND GOLDENSON, ROBERT: The Complete Book of Children's Play. New York, Thomas Y. Crowell Co., 1957.
Although not written about the mentally retarded child, many teachers of the mentally retarded will find this book a source for frequent reference. The age levels indicated will not be applicable to mentally retarded pupils, but the stages of play development indicated will. The book emphasizes play as a part of a child's development and growth. Play activities and materials are discussed. There are extensive lists of games, books, and hobbies; sources of materials and play supplies are also listed.

HUNT, VALERIE V.: Recreation for the Handicapped. New York, Prentice-Hall, Inc., 1955.
This book should be of special help to the teacher who has pupils suffering from handicaps in addition to their mental retardation.

20/

Preparing the Educable Mentally Retarded Child for Adulthood

The teacher should anticipate the future educational needs of the mentally retarded child. In addition to anticipating each pupil's future needs, the teacher should adjust the choice of materials and teaching procedures to prepare the child to live as adult-like as he can. As is true of all children many future needs may only be conjectured, but probable ones should be duly considered. The child's probable environs should be critically eyed. The demands that society will make upon him as an adult should be studied. His training and education should be geared to prepare him to become as well integrated as possible into the communal group of which he will eventually become a part.

Questions to be considered about the future of a mentally retarded child. There are many questions that deserve consideration when planning to help the mentally retarded individual face adulthood as maturely as he can. When chronological maturity has been reached what will his mental maturity be? What about his possible achievements in special abilities, and in traits not strictly intellectual in nature? How well can he be trained to use his hands? What about his mechanical abilities? What about the young woman's homemaking abilities? What about the pupil's personality? How well does he get along with other people? How well does he apply himself to tasks within the scope of his abilities? What will his future milieu probably be? What is the extent of parental concern and understanding? What are the resources for continued guidance after he has left school? Does he possess any physical disabilities that will hinder his activities and adjustments? What vocational, social and recreational opportunities does the community in which he will probably live offer him?

Preparation for acceptance. Preparing the retarded child for adulthood includes preparation for his acceptance by others. Whatever possible should be done to favorably influence the attitudes of those who recognize him as an individual with less than average intellectual abilities. His better performances and traits should be emphasized. Competitive situations, which expose his lack of learning or skills, should be avoided as much as possible, and he should have opportunities to exhibit his better qualities. The mentally retarded child who is accepted by his childhood school and play companions may be expected to find greater acceptance as an adult.

The importance of a good relationship between a special class teacher and co-workers. Before a teacher of the mentally retarded can be of much assistance to pupils in gaining their acceptance as co-workers and playmates by other pupils in the school, he must first gain acceptance as a well-liked and respected member of the school's faculty. It is more likely that, if the teacher of the mentally retarded is well-liked, what he has to say will not be ignored by his co-workers. It takes tact on the part of a teacher of the mentally retarded to gain the cooperative understanding of other teachers. When a request is made of another teacher, such as asking that a retarded pupil be admitted to some regular grade class, the special class teacher should find a way to be of special service to the teacher to whom the request is directed, perhaps taking over some little duty or loaning some special equipment. The teacher should not become a bore by constantly talking about his pupils and their work, but the right word at the right time, said in the right way, will open doors of cooperative understanding. Attitudes of understanding toward the mentally retarded by regular classroom teachers will often be reflected in the attitudes of their pupils toward them.

The attitude of the school principal is important to the success of a special class. Occasionally a principal will be found who looks upon the class or classes for the mentally retarded in his school as being isolated from the rest of the school. To change the attitude of the principal, so that he regards special class pupils as an integral part of the school society, requires considerable tact upon the part of the teacher. The teacher should solicit approval and respect by conforming to the rules set up for the smooth running of the school. Required reports should be free from errors and submitted on time. There should be a readiness to volunteer services where they will be helpful, to serve on committees, and the like. The teacher should refrain from being overly insistent or dogmatic. The teacher should show consideration by bringing problems and requests to the principal at less busy times. When the request for the undertaking of a project has been granted, diligence should be employed to promote its successful fulfillment.

Opportunities should be afforded for association with individuals of normal intelligence. The mentally retarded child of educable degree should have ample opportunity during his school years to associate with children of normal intelligence. In adulthood the educable retarded pupil will be exposed to contact, and often placed in occupational and social competition, with persons more intelligent than himself. During his school years he should not be exposed to the overly competitive atmosphere of a regular classroom, or other competitive situations where he repeatedly encounters defeat, but he should have some opportunities for association with children of normal intelligence in situations where he can achieve a measure of success, and be recognized and accepted as a member of a group.

School opportunities for advancing the social integration of mentally retarded pupils. When, as is a general rule, a special class is located in a school where most of the attendants are of normal intelligence, advantage should be taken of whatever opportunities the school affords to establish satisfying relationships between regular class pupils and pupils who are members of the special class. The retardate who cannot adjust as an adolescent cannot be expected to adjust as an adult. Assuming that the principal or other necessary supervisory authority has approved of these, the following suggestions for helping to establish mutually satisfying relations are offered:

Provided that he is not so over-sized physically that he attracts unpleasant comment, and that he can do the things required about as well as the average kindergartner, a young retardate may be permitted to spend a half hour or so daily with a kindergarten group during some play or game period. With younger children, acceptance in a play group is more dependent upon play age than upon chronological age. Friendships formed may carry over to playground and neighborhood.

A mentally retarded pupil, who is physically equipped to participate and mentally capable of following directions, may be assigned to a gymnasium class with regular grade pupils. To serve its purpose it should be a class in which the retardate does not stand head and shoulders above the rest of the class.

Special class members may learn the school yells and participate as rooters at sports or other school events. A pupil from the regular grades may be invited to come to the special class and teach school yells and songs to its members. The class members may make up yells of their own, and gain prestige by inviting selected pupils to come to their classroom and learn them. In some instances, special class pupils have been selected as cheer leaders for their schools. In one instance a mentally retarded girl was the baton twirler for an organized cheer group.

Assemblies afford opportunities for the school, as a whole, to gain respect for the abilities of special class pupils. A cast may be made only of special class students performing for an audience which includes the regular grades, or spots may be found for one or more special class pupils when a performance is an all-school project.

Backstage jobs, setting up scenery, arranging props, cueing performers, etc., may be shared with pupils from the regular grades. Auditorium seating may need to be arranged. Ushers may be needed. Such tasks have greater value if shared with regular class pupils. It should not appear that a chore has been assigned to a pupil because of his inability to perform tasks of greater difficulty—the task itself should not be stigmatized by always having it assigned only to members of the special class.

A birthday child may be permitted to invite one or two children from the regular grades to his classroom birthday celebration.

When the special class is going on a trip, as many pupils from the regular grades as can be conveniently accommodated and supervised may be invited to go along. The ability of pupils to share and discuss interests should be taken into account in the selection of invited guests. In like manner certain pupils from a special class may be invited to share some of the outings of the regular grades.

When the principal needs two boys to go on an errand or perform some task, one may be selected from the regular grades and one from the special class to do whatever is needed. When choices are made on the basis of compatibility of personality and interests, there is more likelihood that relationships of some degree of permanency may result.

Any extra-curricular activities sponsored by the school, as sports teams, recreational projects, hobby clubs, service clubs, etc., should admit to membership any mental retardate in the school who is qualified to benefit from membership and can perform acceptably.

The playground is where the mental retardates can meet other children without being hampered by academic barriers. In order to better accommodate the play needs of different grade and age groups, when the school offers more than one recess period during a half-day session, pupils in a special class may be recessed at different periods, allowing each pupil to be assigned to the play group that most nearly accommodates his social and recreational needs. Suggestions have previously been offered regarding the supervisory responsibilities of the teacher where one general recess period is the practice.

When the aptitudes of a mentally retarded pupil forecast reasonable success, he may be permitted to attend classes in music, art, industrial arts, home economics, vocational training, or any other class to which he can successfully adapt himself. If he needs a little additional instruction to help him hold his own in a class, he should be furnished this by his classroom teacher.

Sometimes the special class has equipment not available in the regular classroom. When its use might be needed for the completion of some regular classroom projects, one or two pupils might be permitted to come to the special classroom, and use the equipment under the supervision of a special class student familiar with its use. Sometimes other special class students may be called in to help with a project. To illustrate: A primary class needed some chairs and a table for a housekeeping corner in their room. Some of the older retarded boys made the furniture, and some of the children, from the class for which it was intended, worked alongside a few of the younger pupils in the special class to paint the furniture. In another case a fifth grade girl and boy came to the special classroom to help older boys make the scenery and props for an all-school play.

Establishing contacts with out-of-school groups. The teacher of a special class should canvas the community for organized youth groups in which mentally retarded pupils, who are of suitable ages and possess sufficient adaptability, may find membership, and begin to think of themselves as a part of the world outside their homes, school, and neighborhood. A few possible groups are: Boy Scouts, Girl Scouts, Y.M.C.A., Y.W.C.A., 4-H clubs, Little League baseball teams, and church youth groups. The teacher may need to prevail upon family members, schoolmates, youth leaders, church leaders, or other persons to effect the necessary liaison.

Pupils should be aware of what their community has to offer them. Before the retardate leaves school, he should be in possession of information about where he can find wholesome recreation and suitable companions. He should be informed about parks and recreational centers, Y.M.C.A., Y.W.C.A., fraternal organizations, locally sponsored sports teams (which, if ineligible as a player, the retardate may follow as a fan), home demonstration groups, needle work and handicraft clubs which are sometimes sponsored by department stores or commercial organizations, hobby fairs, or any other group which gives him an opportunity to take part. The retardate should be informed about the health, welfare, and employment agencies in his community, and have some idea of when and how to avail himself of their services.

Church connections for the retardate. The province of the public school does not extend to the retardate's religious training, but a teacher may suggest to a parent that a church connection chosen by the parent may be expected to add to the child's moral stature, or at least bring the child into association with persons of good moral habits. If a retardate derives satisfaction from church or Sunday school attendance, and takes part in some church-sponsored social or recreational activities, he may find less need to seek social satisfaction in places of questionable repute, or seek companionship with persons likely to have a poor moral influence upon him. If a parent has no objection to having his child attend church, but is lax in helping him to establish a church connection, with parental permission the teacher may turn to someone to help get the child satisfactorily located, as a neighborhood child and/or a churchgoer. There may be times when a teacher will want to talk to a child's pastor or ask for pastoral help in his guidance.

The retardate and marriage. The interest of society might be served better if the retardate did not marry and did not have children, but the school cannot inculcate the retardate against marriage and parenthood. Advice intended to either discourage marriage or directly prepare for marriage is a matter that should be deferred until a retardate has reached a marriageable age, and then only if he or she is contemplating marriage or at least has shown signs of interest in marriage. If the teacher has the problem forced upon his attention by a pupil, an earnest effort should be made to locate a qualified counselor.

Responsibility of the school for preparation for marriage. Although advice concerning marriage is something that belongs to a retardate's after-school years, he may be fortified in a general way to better meet the problems of marriage and parenthood. The female retardate may be trained to be as good a homemaker as she can, including training in the care of children, to the extent that she may be expected to make use of the things taught her. The male retardate may be trained to earn as good a livelihood as he can, and learn how to do necessary household chores, and keep a home in decent repair. He needs to learn to have concern for all members of a household of which he is a part. He should be helped to build up a set of habits and attitudes that will be worthy of emulation by the children he may bear, because setting good examples will be his most effective means of teaching.

The teacher as a confidante. During his school years a child's feeling of security may be strengthened if he has someone with whom he can talk freely about himself and his problems. The teacher should be easily available as that someone. Minor though his problems may appear to others, they may be of major importance to him. If, by listening to a pupil's petty problems, the teacher has become established in the child's mind as his confidante, he will be apt to continue coming to his confidante with his problems as he approaches adulthood. There are some boy-girl problems of social and ethical significance that bear discussion in open classroom forum, but problems of an intimate and personal nature should be reserved for private discussion. During the retardate's last year in school, regular counseling periods should be provided for the discussion of future plans as well as current problems.

Provision for continued guidance after leaving school. In schools where guidance and counseling service are provided for retarded pupils, the responsibility of the teacher is one of cooperation. Where guidance and counseling are not provided, the majority of special class pupils will depend upon their teachers to give them whatever assistance they can in making the transition from school life to adult life. The time will never come in the life of even a well-adjusted mental retardate when he will be entirely free from the need for some measure of guidance. Guidance may be needed when he is embarking on some new adventure, when some new-found acquaintance is attempting to untowardly influence his actions, when some unforeseen difficulty has arisen, when any situation is presented wherein established ways and habits of behavior are inapplicable or inadequate, where promises of reward blind him to the wisdom of his actions, or when a problem is too complicated for him to solve alone. While a retardate is still in school, the teacher may call in some individual who might serve as a mentor to sit in at counseling periods, thus establishing in the mind of the retardate the idea that the person called in is one who is interested in his welfare; or arrangements might be made with a sympathetic and wise person to have the retardate visit him to talk over some recreational, social, employment, or behavior problem.

More than one contact should be made. It is advisable to establish more than one contact so that the individual will not be left without a confidante in case of withdrawal of an individual counselor. Of course, he should not have so many advisors that he takes the same problem to all of them, and perhaps receives conflicting and confusing advice; however, he can profit from the help of two or three individuals if they are concerned with different phases of his needs and interests. The best counselor a retardate can have is an intelligent and interested member of his own family, but there will be many retardates who cannot look to their homes for wise advice. Suggested counselors are: the pastor or pastor's assistant of the church attended by the retardate, a kindly housewife who may be in need of household assistance, a sympathetically inclined business man who can provide or help a retardate find employment, a recreational or social worker, a "big brother" or a "big sister," a doctor in whom the retardate has confidence, or any person with wisdom and understanding who may be willing to listen to the retardate's problems and give advice as needed.

SUGGESTED READING

The Adolescent Exceptional Child (1954); The Exceptional Child Faces Adulthood (1955). The Woods Schools, Langhorne, Pennsylvania.

These two pamphlets contain conference proceedings of the Child Research Clinic of the Woods Schools. They contain addresses and panel discussions by doctors, psychologists and educators. The topic of the 1954 conference was "The Adolescent Child, a Realistic Approach to Treatment and Training." The topic of the 1955 conference was "The Exceptional Child Faces Adulthood."

21/

The Teacher of the Mentally Retarded and the Community

The teacher should be an active member of the community. Any teacher of retardates who are approaching adulthood needs to be an active member of the community in which he lives and works. The teacher needs to be known as an individual who is interested in the community and its membership. While the teacher should not become involved in so many time-consuming projects that teaching efficiency is affected adversely, there should be a readiness to assume a just and proportionate share of community responsibility.

The teacher's influence upon the acceptance of retardates as members of the community. Just for a teacher to be a well-liked person in a community has its influence upon communal attitudes towards mentally retarded individuals. The teacher can influence attitudes by talking to the right people at the right time and place. Opportunities to build up favorable attitudes should not be overlooked but it should also be remembered that prolixity may find unwilling listeners. The community tends to transfer its respect and liking for the teacher to respect and liking for his pupils.

The teacher of the mentally retarded and the parents. The first members of the community with whom the teacher should seek contact are the child's parents. The teacher needs to know the parents if the child is to be well-understood. He needs to know something about the kind of home from which the child comes. He needs to know the parents' attitude toward their offspring and the child's retardation. Perhaps the parents recognize the child's handicap; perhaps they do not. Perhaps they accept their child as he is; perhaps they resent or reject him.

The teacher's attitude on first contact with a parent. While the teacher will want to gain as much information as he can to increase his understanding of a child, the talk with one or both parents or a visit to the home should not be made a quiz session. Questions regarding family background, medical history of the child, etc., may create resentment, and a resentful parent is not a cooperative one. A better attitude to take is that the teacher will appreciate being told anything either parent believes will be helpful. It is generally wise to get the parent to talk as much as he will with as little questioning as possible. When the parent talks freely and voluntarily, the observant teacher can learn much about the relationship between parent and child, and can learn much about why the child is the kind of child he is. It is wise to let a parent expose his attitudes before any attempt is made to influence them. After the teacher and the parent become better acquainted and if a proper rapport has been established, the school and the home can be of much help to each other.

The parents ask "Why?" It is, of course, desirable that the examining psychologist, a social worker, or other qualified person prepare the parents for their child's enrollment in a special class. Sometimes it is the teacher who must answer the parents' question, "Why should our child be placed in a special class?" Such a question needs to be answered tactfully. Some parents

can be told more than others, according to their ability to comprehend what is said and the wisdom with which imparted information will be used. Some parents can intelligently interpret what is said, but others cannot be depended upon to do so.
Some parents can look at the situation with some degree of
objectivity while others cannot.

Explaining a child's placement. The inability to progress
academically is always a truthful and understandable answer
to the parents' questions regarding a child's placement in a
special class. It can be pointed out that by putting a child in a
special class the child will be spared the embarrassment of
grade repetition. The enrollment in a special class is less than
that of the regular grades. The teacher will have the time to
give the child the individual attention he needs. It can be
pointed out to the parents that their child is no different from
many others and there are many children who learn more
slowly than the average. It should be pointed out also that the
child's teacher will be trained to know how to help slow learners, and how to make the most of their abilities. The fact that
the child will have a much better opportunity to do his best in
a special class should be emphasized.

*The parents ask, "How long will our child have to stay in
the special class?"* The parents are often concerned with the
return of their child to the regular grades as soon as possible,
and they should be told frankly that only occasionally is a
child returned to the regular grades. It should be pointed out
that the child's former classmates go along at their regular
pace, and the academic gap between them and the retarded
child grows no less, and that even though the child is making
consistent progress, he cannot be returned to his regular class.
To put him with a class of children much younger than
himself would be unfair. It should be pointed out that the child
will receive instruction in certain practical subjects which
would not be available to him in the regular grades, but which
are of importance to him. Usually if increments in learning are
pointed out for the parents, they will be convinced that their
child is making progress.

Parents ask "What is our child's IQ?" Parents, to whom IQ is a familiar term, may ask the teacher to reveal their child's IQ. Not all parents are equipped to use such information wisely. Whether or not the parents should be informed is usually a decision for the psychologist to make. Generally it is better for the teacher to inform the parents that it is not the policy of the school to reveal the IQ's of its pupils. The teacher can talk to the parents in general terms about rates of learning and levels of achievement. Limitations may be indicated as far as is necessary to keep parents from demanding too much from their child, and the potentialities that deserve nurturing should be emphasized.

Preserving the interest of the parents. The more the parents participate in the affairs of the special class and of the school, the more they are apt to learn about their child and his specific needs. A parent may bake cup cakes for a school party; two or three mothers may furnish transportation for a school excursion; parents may come to see their children perform at a school program. The teacher may help to form a parents' organization, and as the parents get together and talk about their children's problems, they become more hopeful, and take on a sense of responsibility for their part in helping pupils live as normally as possible as members of the community. Meeting with other parents affords opportunity to communicate the idea of community acceptance of the retardate. The more intelligent the parent membership, the less responsibility the teacher will have for holding a parent group together. When the unit can be organized as a part of the regular P.T.A., so much the better.

The IQ of a pupil is not the concern of the community. The teacher of a class for mentally retarded children should refrain from publicly discussing the IQ's of the pupils. The IQ of a pupil is a matter of personal concern to be treated confidentially by the teacher and he should not reveal it even to fellow teachers. The IQ should be revealed only when knowledge of it will result in constructive assistance to the child. The IQ range for admittance to a class may be a matter of general knowledge in the community, but the teacher has a duty to protect pupils against prejudicial judgments by treating their individual IQ's confidentially. The children's own accomplishments will identify them as slow learners, but there is no need to publicly tag them with their IQ's.

Effect of class nomenclature on the public. Many people in the community will know of the existence of classes for slow learning children in the community, and many will know specific children who attend such classes. The nomenclature of classes for the educable mentally retarded differs from community to community. Classes for the trainable mentally retarded are usually quite frankly called "classes for the mentally retarded." Since the educable mentally retarded child will usually become a part of the social structure of the community, names for classes for them are usually camouflaged in some manner to prevent stigmatization. At a White House Conference, the committee recommended the use of the term "Special Classes," and further recommended that terms, as "Primary, Intermediate, Advanced, or Special A, or Special B," also be used. These classes also have been called Opportunity Classes and Development Classes, and in some instances are known only by a room number or a teacher's name. Whatever the method of identification, children soon are recognized as slow learners. The assistance of the community will be needed in helping graduates of special classes become successfully integrated into society; this can be accomplished effectively provided that there is also understanding on the part of the community. Names for special classes should be chosen carefully, but, more than that, attitudes toward the slow learning child should be molded in a manner to assure his kindly and understanding acceptance as a member of the community.

The public asks questions about the special class. When members of the community ask the teacher questions about a special class, they deserve truthful, but impersonal, answers of a general nature. Some typical questions and possible answers are:

Which children attend the special class? *Answer:* Those children who learn academic subjects so slowly that, if left in the regular grades, they become grade repeaters.

What about their IQ's? *Answer:* The IQ's of *trainable* children run considerably lower than the IQ's of most of us. The IQ's of *educable* retardates are not so low. There may be no more difference between the IQ of a person of good average intelligence and that of an educable retarded child, than between the former person and that of an individual rated as gifted in intelligence.

What is the IQ? *Answer:* The IQ is a comparative measure of intelligence. It applies to intellectual abilities; it *does not* measure mechanical, motor, musical or artistic abilities nor personality or social traits.

How does the special class differ from the regular grades? *Answer:* The enrollment in the special class is relatively small, so that a teacher has time to give each pupil individual attention. The child is taught things of greatest importance first. He is taught many practical things which will make him a better homemaker, worker, and citizen.

What kind of personalities do retarded children have? *Answer:* Children in special classes differ as widely in their personalities as do children in regular classes. They possess no specific personality traits. Special class training emphasizes the inculcation of desirable personality traits.

Talks to community groups. The teacher of the mentally retarded may be called upon to speak before community groups. Remarks should be chosen to fit the group for which they are intended. A talk to a businessmen's organization should differ from one to parents of the mentally retarded. The potentialities and better qualities of retarded pupils should be stressed, but there should be no false claims made for nonexistent attainments. The answers to questions in the preceding paragraphs may suggest areas for discussion. The responsibilties of community members in helping retardates make worthwhile community adjustments should be pointed out and explained. The fact that the retardate's maturity depends upon acceptance by the community should be stressed. In certain situations it may be desirable to suggest the need for volunteers to help with recreational or guidance programs or to help find employment for a retardate.

Follow-up work for the retardate. The retardate should have guidance if he is to get from the community all that it has to offer him, and if he is to give to the community all that he can. Only in a limited number of school organizations is there any provision made for guidance and follow-up work for the mental retardate after he leaves school. Lacking such help, the teacher should make such contacts as are possible with employment agencies, social agencies, and individuals who may be of assistance with guidance problems. Making provisions for moral guidance after the pupil leaves school has been discussed previously.

The community and the retardate must be prepared for each other. As has been emphasized at different points in this book, the retardate should be taught those skills and knowledges and habits and attitudes that will enable him to live as adultlike as he can as a member of the community. He should know what the community has to offer him vocationally, recreationally, and socially. He should be taught to assume as much responsibility as he can for making and keeping his community a healthful, safe, and pleasant place in which to live. The members of the community need to be prepared to understand the needs and potentialities, as well as recognize the limitations, of the retardate, so that he may be afforded opportunities for success, without demanding from him more than he is able to give. The retardate and his fellow citizens need to be introduced to each other, and learn their responsibilities to each other, so that they may learn to live cooperatively together. The retardate needs to be prepared for society, and society needs to be prepared for him. The dimensions of the special classroom extend far beyond its four containing walls, and the teacher of the mental retardate needs to be a teacher of the community as well as the child.

SUGGESTED READING

Ecob, Katherine G.: The Retarded Child in the Community. New York, New York State Society for Mental Health, 1955.
A sociological approach to the needs and problems of the retarded child in the community.

DAVIS, STANLEY POWELL: The Mentally Retarded in Society. New York, Columbia University Press, 1959.

Another sociological treatise which presents some of the problems imposed upon society and upon the individual by mental retardation, and adaptive measures that are sometimes employed.

General References

KIRK, SAMUEL and JOHNSON, O.: Educating the Retarded Child. Boston, Houghton Mifflin Co., 1951.

This book furnishes a good over-all picture of the education of the mentally retarded. It reviews and summarizes past and present educational procedures and programs. Sources of materials and supplies are listed. Appended to the book is an extensive and well-annotated bibliography.

WALLIN, J. E. WALLACE: Education of the Mentally Handicapped. New York, Harper and Brothers, 1955.

This book is a complete and well-documented work that will furnish the teacher with a good general background in the field of the education of the mentally retarded. It deals with the historical background of education for the retarded, points out the needs for special education, stresses the need for educational adjustments to meet the individual needs, and the educational procedures required. It acquaints the teacher with methods of identification. A chapter is devoted to the discussion of the implications and consequences of mental deficiency. An extensive bibliography is included.

WEBER, ELMER W.: Educable and Trainable Mentally Retarded Children. Chapter 6. Finding, Screening, Diagnosing, and Placing the Mentally Retarded. Springfield, Ill., Charles C Thomas, 1962.

This chapter indicates the roles of teachers, psychometrists, psychologists, physicians, and social workers in locating and properly placing the mentally retarded child.

ROTHSTEIN, JEROME H.: Mental Retardation: Readings and Resources. New York, Holt, Rinehart and Winston, 1961.

This book furnishes an excellent guide for the teacher who wants to become informed about the viewpoints of specialists in the field of mental retardation.

Periodicals

CHILDREN LIMITED. Published by The National Association for Retarded Children, 386 Park Avenue South, New York.

The N.A.R.C. is an organization founded by parents, and a very large percentage of its members are parents. It has chapters located all over the United States. Children Limited is the news and informational periodical of the organization.

COOPERATIVE RESEARCH PROJECTS. Issued by the U. S. Department of Health, Education, and Welfare, Office of Education, Washington, D. C.

This is an annual publication which reports on research projects, including those on mental retardation, which are being conducted under grants from the U. S. Office of Education.

TRAINING SCHOOL BULLETIN. Published by The Training School, Vineland, New Jersey.

This periodical contains many informative articles of interest to the teacher of the mentally retarded.

JOURNAL OF EXCEPTIONAL CHILDREN. Published by the International Council for Exceptional Children, 1201 16th St., Washington 6, D. C.

This publication carries articles of interest to teachers of exceptional children, including the mentally retarded.

Appendix

As the public is becoming increasingly aware of the needs of the mentally retarded, state and local governmental agencies are expanding their programs of service. Many state departments of public instruction have specialists in the field of mental retardation on their staffs, as do many city and county school systems. Subject to compliance with specific standards, many states provide financial aid to help local school systems with the payment of teachers' salaries and the cost of maintenance of special classes for the mentally retarded.

By 1949 laws on the statutes of twenty-four states authorized the establishment of special classes for the mentally retarded. By 1959 forty-eight states had such legislation.

As well as providing consultative services the stronger state programs set up standards for (a) pupil admission to special classes, (b) certification of special class teachers, and (c) selection of curricular materials.

During the last ten years the federal government has become increasingly active in the field of mental retardation. Congress has passed laws which provide for the development of important programs in the fields of health, welfare and education of the mentally retarded. Funds have been created to establish fellowships for promising individuals to prepare them for positions as supervisors and directors of educational programs at state and local levels, and instructors or directors in colleges and universities which train teachers of the mentally retarded.

Federal grants to provide financial aid, including aid for edu cational services, are available to states who qualify on the basis of their present programs for the mentally retarded. Grants are also available to aid universities, colleges and local school systems (through state educational agencies) for educational research in the field of mental retardation.

Index